institute of
financial services
School of Finance

Understanding the Contact Centre Environment

2nd Edition

David Mack & Claire Bateson

2nd Edition by Claire Bateson

The *ifs* is the official brand of

Institute of Financial Services
IFS House
4-9 Burgate Lane
Canterbury
Kent
CT1 2XJ
United Kingdom

T   01227 818649
F   01227 479641
E   editorial@ifslearning.com
W   www.ifslearning.com

Institute of Financial Services publications are published by The Chartered Institute of Bankers, a non-profit making registered educational charity.

The Chartered Institute of Bankers believes that the sources of information upon which the book is based are reliable and has made every effort to ensure the complete accuracy of the text. However, neither CIB, the author nor any contributor can accept any legal responsibility whatsoever for consequences that may arise from errors or omissions or any opinion or advice given.

Typeset by Etica Press Ltd, Malvern
Printed by Thomson Litho, East Kilbride, Scotland.

Contents

Contents

Contents

Unit 1

Contact centres as part of organizational strategy

The aim of this unit is to enable you to state the key issues affecting organizations, which led to the contact centre concept.

This unit is to help you understand why contact centres are used by organizations to reach their customers and the vital part they play in the communication process. It will give you a context in which the remainder of this text sits.

The rise in the popularity of contact centres is due partly because consumers wanted to access information and their financial service provider more easily and in different ways to suit their needs. Coupled with this was the increasingly high cost of providers meeting these needs in a traditional way through the branch network. Fortunately advances in technology have enabled new ways of communication and working to be achieved.

Contact centres already existed in some form in the home shopping sector, simply by groups of people answering calls in the same 'hunt group'. A hunt group is where the telephone system passes a call to another operator in the same linked network of phones after a pre-set numbers of rings. The consumer would just use one external telephone number to be connected to any number of operators within this linked network. These operators probably didn't see themselves as contact centre advisers and often performed other clerical duties within an office.

This unit explores how an organization formulates its strategic direction and the process it may go through to achieve this. You will see what process an organization goes through to pinpoint where changes are required. We will then look at changing consumer buying habits that led to some of these changes in the financial services industry and how technology can meet these needs. This new technology has led to the creation of new ways of delivering service to the consumers and inevitably financial services providers compete to attract their share of this market. We will explore how this competition has created a very dynamic and competitive market place for financial services and products.

1.1 Setting strategic direction

The top team of many large organizations will spend time considering where the organization is going in terms of its overall business aims. This will result in a coherent approach that can be communicated to investors, employees and the stock market. This will be in the form of various aims and can be known as 'corporate strategies' or 'strategic objectives'. These strategic objectives will seem quite high level, however for a complex organization, with many parts, it gives a starting point for determining what the operational and tactical objectives within the organization should be.

Think

> What is a strategic objective?

A strategic objective is one which:

- affects the long-term direction of an organization – typically around three to five years;
- tries to achieve a competitive advantage for the organization;
- is concerned with the scope of the organization's activities – for instance should it stay in a particular industry sector or move into another one? Should it take over another organization to acquire a business in another area?
- matches the organization's activities to the business and economic environment in which it operates and the consumers it serves. This is sometimes known as the 'strategic fit'.

Think

> What are the issues that could be considered as strategic?

Strategic issues are ones that relate to the:

- overall organizational structure and its management style;
- relationship with the government and other external interest groups;
- acquisition of new businesses or divestment of parts of the existing business;
- national and international reputation and relationships;
- culture of the organization and key people issues;
- past or anticipated technological innovations.

1.1.1 *How does an organization formulate its corporate strategies?*

An organization will formulate its strategy, ie decide what to do, by following a process. This could be as in Figure 1:

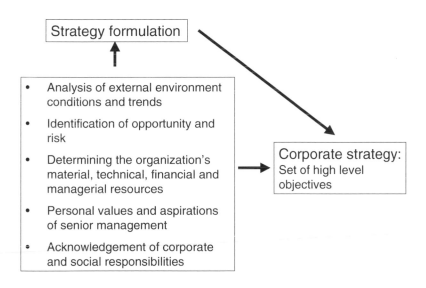

Figure 1: *Formulating corporate strategy (amended from Kenneth R Andrews)*

Once these corporate strategies have been determined, the various business units can then be engaged in what they can do to support the achievement of these aims. This will result in the formulation of shorter-term operational objectives, typically with a one to two-year time horizon. This process is likely to entail changes within the organization, however. In some cases this can have far reaching implications such as:

- **major resource changes** in the organization. This can be in terms of premises, staffing levels, organizational structures or choice of suppliers;
- **operational decisions**, which could include management and control, geographic spread, processes and procedures, distribution policies, marketing and advertising and human resource policies;
- **values and expectations of stakeholders** – stakeholders are the different groups of people who have an interest in the organization and its activities. Most commonly these are shareholders, management, the workforce, unions, consumers, suppliers and the local community.

The effective implementation of any changes is important as many of the stakeholder groups find change unsettling, particularly if they perceive the change to have an adverse affect on them. Whilst a change in strategic direction, for example a move from high street branch presence to contact centre delivered service, may seem to meet the needs of an organization and its customers, the implementation of such a change can be quite hard for a large organization due to its size to change direction quickly. Think of how difficult it is to stop an ocean-going liner compared with a rowing boat. This implementation phase must be considered carefully as part of the strategy formulation. In the fast changing world of financial services, however, many providers have felt they had no choice but to try to change direction quickly and provide customers with more and better technology-based solutions.

1.2 The changing needs of consumers

New corporate strategies will generally be devised in response to the external business and social environment. This environment falls into a number of areas for example:

- political climate and changes both nationally and internationally;
- economic stability;
- social and consumer trends;
- technological innovation;
- legal parameters in which society works; and
- environmental challenges such as pollution and waste disposal.

Consumers form part of the external business and social environment and we will now have an overview of the consumers' role in each of these areas.

1.2.1 *Political*

The Conservative party had the majority in government from 1979–1997. In 1997 the Labour party won the General Election following dissatisfaction with Conservative party policies. Whenever a new party takes over there will always be a period of settling in and changes made. Even so every year the government of the day will introduce changes to taxes, benefits and policies that affect many of the population. We are obviously also exposed to European politics and the UK's relationship with America frequently means that the country's politicians are at the centre of the world's stage as the Middle Eastern conflicts have shown. The consumer can be affected by such problems both at home and abroad. If there are wars, for example, people do not feel so confident and therefore are less likely to spend and take unnecessary risks with their money.

1.2.2 *Economic*

The 'economy' is a term used to describe the financial system that the government and analysts use to gauge the wealth of the country. At the time of writing (April 2004) the economy was going through a period of low inflation and low interest rates, which also means slow growth and low unemployment. In this situation people who are reliant on income from their investments are not happy because the return they are getting on their capital is low.

On the other hand home owners are keen to borrow as much as possible against their property because the repayments seem affordable and it is a more immediate way of obtaining funds than saving. Additionally, when the housing market is booming, consumer confidence tends to be high. Borrowing is not just limited to homeowners, most students are in debt by the time they leave university and overall consumer borrowing continues to grow.

Think

What if the opposite was true and the economy had high interest rates and high inflation?

In the 1980s there were high interest rates and high inflation, prices rose out of line with the rises in people's salaries. The stock market grew in value and investors were happy as they could see good returns for their money. The housing boom spiralled out of control, however, and the market crashed, leaving many homeowners with negative equity and high repayments that they found hard to afford. We are today seeing that stock market-based investments, such as endowments, do not necessarily bring the returns they promised when people took out the policies 20 years ago, as these policies are not reaching their projected end values.

1.2.3 *Social*

The population is ageing, ie there are more older people than young people – this is the same in the rest of Europe too. Young people are spending longer in education and statistics show that those with qualifications are more likely to find work. This means, however, that there are less and less people paying into government schemes for pensions, and funds for services such as health and education are stretched too. People are worried that there won't be sufficient public funds to care for them in their old age. There are more single parent families, people living alone rather than marrying, and more elderly people living alone. This means that the demand for housing is increasing and this pushes prices up. This is one of the reasons why first time buyers find it hard to get onto the housing ladder.

With more women working and people leading busier lifestyles, few have time for queuing in shops and banks. Many also prefer a 'one-stop-shop' and the supermarkets have been able to take advantage of this by introducing products that are outside their traditional range of groceries. The increase in shift working to fit around family commitments means people need to be able to access services outside normal office hours. This has lead to 24/7 working and opening hours. Lifestyle surveys have also found that over 85% of the population watch TV everyday, which suggests that people spend a lot of their leisure time at home.

Question

What do consumers want from their financial services provider that fits in with their lifestyle?

Consumers want a service that fits in with their busy lifestyle. So this will be access to information when they want it, and convenience, so not just when the bank branch is open. The ability to have this access from the comfort of their home is also desirable particularly if that interaction with their provider is quick, easy and efficient. Consumers also want value for money and many do not see the need to pay for banking services.

1.2.4 *Technological*

There have been rapid developments in technology since the middle of the last century. Computers are becoming smaller and much cheaper to produce. As more people buy computers the unit costs go down. The ability to carry different forms of data has increased and this medium has gone from copper wire to optical fibre cables and now wireless communication is the norm. Almost every household has a fixed telephone line and over 75% of people have mobile phones, which means that for the moment this will be most consumers' preferred method of communication.

The Internet has been a breakthrough that enables consumers' access and convenience to view a range of suppliers at the same time which gives an added benefit of choice. This has enabled people to browse and shop when they want to and to communicate with a supplier about their purchase. Nearly half of the population have access to the Internet from a home PC which means that this form of communication will increase. People are becoming more accepting of new technology and when a new development is made a consumer is more likely to try it rather than wait until their friends already have it.

1.2.5 *Legal*

There are many laws and practices that govern the social framework of this country. They are there to protect people and to ensure some sort of order within our society. There are those that are for the welfare of employees such as the Minimum Wage and Minimum Working Hours legislation. There are some laws that protect the consumer such as the Supply of Goods and Services Acts 1982 and the Consumer Credit Act 1974. As part of the European Union we are now affected by those laws created by the European Community: the recent Human Rights Act (1998) was an example of this. In the financial services industry the Financial Services and Markets Act 2000 continues the pattern of increased regulation as mortgages and general insurance sales fall under the auspices of the single regulator, the Financial Services Authority.

1.2.6 *Environmental*

In developed countries where there is a high demand for energy, a large transport network and large numbers of people living in concentrated numbers in towns and cities there will always be environmental pressures. This type of living does have an impact on the place in which we live, in terms of carbon dioxide emissions (which are toxic) and the disposal of waste to name but two. Consumers can actively decide to support those organizations that have a good environmental policy and undertake their own recycling and energy saving activities themselves. People are becoming more aware of the problems created by the modern lifestyle and more willing to support schemes that take care of their living space.

1.3 The growth of new technology

In section 1.2 we had an overview of the consumers' reaction to the growth of technology and nowadays more people are keen to embrace the benefits this can bring. In this section we will look in outline at how technology has changed in contact centres and some of the challenges this has posed to organizations that use technology to help them deliver products and services to consumers.

Traditionally, contact centres were based on voice communication and postal services. As the systems that managed the calls in contact centres became more sophisticated, Automatic Call Distributors (ACDs) were used and these also evolved to handle more complex situations. The ACD is a computerized system that routes the incoming calls to the next available agent in the hunt group, preferably the one that has been in 'idle' the longest. The next step was to use Interactive Voice Response (IVR) which is a computer interface to a telephone line that handles the call and Computer Telephony Integration (CTI) to pre-handle calls and route them to available advisers with the right skill set, or indeed handle calls fully without any human involvement. More intelligent software means that more elements of the service can be automated leaving advisers to deal with more complex tasks.

The Internet has enabled organizations to develop websites and e-mail for consumer contact. Customers can now manage their accounts themselves rather than by telephoning an adviser to have the transaction done for them and can in effect 'self-service'.

Fortunately in the UK much of the telephone network has been upgraded to a digital system. This means that many telephone users can use either Integrated Services Digital Network (ISDN), or more increasingly, broadband connections for fast Internet and e-mail services. This makes it cheaper and quicker for consumers to use these forms of communication to interact their financial services provider. Wireless Application Protocol (WAP), General Packet Radio Service (GPRS) and Personal Digital Applications (PDA) make this interaction available for people on the move and those people that like to have the latest gadget.

Whilst the telephone remains the medium of choice for many consumers these additional ways of communicating are more attractive as home computers become cheaper to buy and the cost of 'surfing' the Internet lowers.

Question

What sort of challenges does this growth in technology create for organizations?

1.3.1 *Challenges*

There are a number of challenges faced by organizations, which are outlined as follows.

- When installing system there will always be a cost implication, which should be researched and scoped fully. Sometimes it is cheaper to start from scratch rather than to try to add a 'bolt-on' to an existing system. There will be the additional cost of updates and maintenance. Consideration should also be given to the possibility of interruption to customer service whilst the new system is being put into place. Thought should be given as to how existing data will be transferred to the new system; will this in turn mean additional cost?

- Systems reliability – will it work? Sufficient testing needs to be undertaken before going live and many new innovations are resisted because organizations feel that the risk of failure is too high. Disaster recovery planning will always be important for any organization, as business interruption due to a computer failure is highly undesirable.

- Will the staff have the right skill set when media changes, eg from voice to e-mail? If monotonous tasks are taken away are they able to problem solve? Recruitment and selection of appropriate staff is important, as is training and re-training when required. This again means additional cost to the organization.

- Customer acceptance of new technologies whilst more of a challenge in the past still can be a problem today. Let's not forget that the majority of customers do prefer voice-based contact.

- Security of websites and databases is paramount, particularly in the financial services industry. Consumers need to know that on-line transactions are secure, otherwise the trust they have in their provider and the Internet, as a means of communication, will be broken. There will always be scams by criminals to acquire passwords and consumers will be alarmed by breaches of confidentiality in whatever form.

- The ongoing need to reduce and contain costs has lead to the outsourcing of contact centre operations overseas. At the time of writing it is not yet clear whether this will bring long-term cost reductions, however the short-term view is that the saving on staff salaries is worth while.

Organizations cannot afford to stand still as other providers with newer technology can easily take business away from them. A watchful eye always needs to be kept on the competition to see what they are offering and to try to match or better it. If an organization is able to make cost reductions *and* improve overall service then they have a competitive advantage on the remainder of the field.

1.4 New delivery channels

A 'delivery channel' is the term given to how an organization enables consumers to access its services and therefore how the organization makes a route to its chosen markets. Different industries will use different delivery channels depending on their products, services and customer base. In financial services the traditional delivery channel is the branch, known also as 'bricks and mortar', which is used to encompass face-to-face, post and telephone contact, delivered by staff at a customer's local branch. This gave the traditional branch high levels of autonomy in a de-centralized organization, in times when the banking industry was not as competitive as it is today.

There were some problems with this, in that the lack of central control led to increased costs, poor lending decisions led to bad debt and losses and local processing practises that were costly to operate and as they were outside standard procedures and difficult to monitor. It was a very resource-hungry way of accommodating customers and frequently led to customer complaints when things went wrong. The counter service for cashing customer cheques was also resource-hungry as the cashier was the only point of access for the customer. In many branches queries and questions even for simple information such as account balances caused queues.

In an effort to reduce costs and reduce in-branch waiting a new service was developed – the Automatic Teller Machine (ATM). The forerunners of those we know today were introduced in 1971 from America. These were very basic at first and did not have a link to the main computer databases but they did provide a new delivery channel that customers could use for basic services outside normal office hours. As they became more sophisticated the variety of tasks they could perform increased which gave customers services they needed. As the ATMS became online to the main customer database the banks were more easily able to decline cash to those who did not have sufficient funds in their accounts, which in turn reduced the costs of managing overdrawn accounts and saved time with in-branch enquiries. The ATMs were branch-based but these days they can be found in places such as stations, shopping malls and motorway services. They have remained limited in functionality, as new technology has enabled more sophisticated delivery channels to develop. Also the reliance on cash has diminished as consumers become more accustomed to using plastic cards to settle bills.

A number of banks tried to introduce the telephone as a new delivery channel as research showed that fewer and fewer people were going into branches on a regular basis. From an organizational perspective branches were seen to be delivering poor service at a high cost with little profitability. The first telephone bank to be a real success, and remain so today, is First Direct. It was launched in 1989 and, whilst a subsidiary of Midland Bank (now HSBC), it had no branch presence and initially communication was predominantly by phone with postal back up. These early forms of telephone banking were known as 'call centres' rather than contact centres because the reliance was on telephone contact rather than any other form of contact.

At the same time as the new call centres were emerging the financial services industry was going through a period of rapid change and increased competition. The Financial Services Act 1986 (now replaced by the Financial Service and Markets Act 2000) had thrown the doors open to new competitors in the market and the face of the industry was to change forever. To control costs many of the banks centralized activities such as processing and back-office functionality. From a customer view it didn't really matter where the processing was done, so long as it was done. This led to telephone contact also being centralized too and the call centre became a major delivery channel in its own right for many organizations. Branch closures followed in an attempt to make cost reductions and branch staff with experience were recruited into the new call centres.

In the last ten years the Internet has been the largest new delivery channel to emerge and it has been said by some that this will be the death of the contact centre industry. It is likely, however, that the opposite will be the case as contact centres continue to embrace new technology and include it in their delivery channel proposition. This is how call centres have now moved to now being known as 'contact' centres, as consumers can use any means of contact they wish to interact with the centre. Linked to a website, contact centres can add this to their area of responsibility, although to the customer it will simply seem like another way of interacting with the organization. It is now possible for customers to view their account information, undertake their own transactions, transfer money, set up and amend standing orders and interact with their provider by e-mail.

The first real 'virtual' bank that was reliant on a web presence is Egg, a subsidiary of the Prudential Group. Launched in 1998, Egg's proposition was to offer higher interest rates for deposits and competitive interest rates for borrowers based on the fact that there were no traditional costs tied up in bricks and mortar. Whilst the initial success in gaining market share was impressive it has taken some time for Egg to become profitable.

Behind the scenes contact centre technology still moves forward as software becomes more involved in routing and handling calls and assisting advisers to deal with customer queries. Ironically the branch is enjoying resurgence in popularity as customers benefit from the choice of integrated delivery channels now available, now known as 'clicks and mortar'. As consumer needs become diverse and the availability of choice becomes more important these various delivery channels will all play a part in meeting consumer needs.

1.5 Competition

In this final section of the chapter we will examine the effect of increased competition in the financial services industry and some of the more recent developments that has brought this about. The contact centre plays a key role in this competitive environment as it enables many organizations to offer low cost service to the mass-market customer base in an efficient way.

One thing that is a given within this very dynamic industry is that change and competition are constant. As already mentioned in section 1.4, the Financial Services Act 1986 marked the start of increased competition. It meant that the demarcation lines between banks, building societies and insurance companies were removed and each could pursue the market of each other and offer the products and services of the other. This led to a number of building societies and insurance companies de-mutualising, ie ownership of the organization was transferred from the members to shareholders in order to access capital from the stock market. This enabled them to expand their operations into these new areas. The opportunities for growth seemed good.

This increased competition, whilst seemingly good for the consumer, did have its downsides in that some sellers of services did not act appropriately and there have been some 'mis-selling' scandals particularly in the areas of investments and life assurance (although the latter is not simply due to increased competition). This has led to tighter restrictions being imposed on the sale of financial products and the creation of a single regulator, the Financial Services Authority. Generally, however, competition is deemed to be healthy and should increase choice for the consumer.

As this appeared to be a lucrative area, new players to the market emerged that did not have a traditional financial services background. The most prominent of these were the supermarkets who were not held back by a network of unsuitable buildings in inconvenient locations but had premises with plenty of car parking and transport links. They had a fresh approach to marketing financial services that seemed to be easily accessible to all. Today we see financial services products being sold in the supermarket aisles – readily available to shoppers on their weekly visit. There is no longer the stigma and worry of having to visit the bank manager to access services or the wait in the long queue in the banking hall.

After a period of growth it has been only natural that it could not continue at such a pace and over the last few years we have seen a number of mergers and acquisitions occur within the industry.

Think

Which organizations have merged or acquired a competitor?

Examples of this are Royal Bank of Scotland's takeover of NatWest, HSBC taking over Midland, Lloyds and TSB merging with the acquisition of Cheltenham and Gloucester Building Society and Halifax Building Society merging with Bank of Scotland to make HBoS. The benefits of this are numerous:

- cost control and economies of scale as back office processing operations are merged;
- acquisition of new customers and increase market share that would have taken considerable marketing and sales effort to achieve under normal circumstances;
- acquisition of customers in new markets with different products. These customers can then be cross-sold other products;
- acquisition of intellectual property that belongs to the acquired organization and therefore gain new expertise to strengthen the new organization;
- move into new geographical areas in which there is no existing representation;
- acquisition of new technology and systems that are deemed to be leading edge;
- acquisition staff skills and knowledge that can grow the new business.

This consolidation in the industry has also enabled organizations to divest those parts of their operation that were unprofitable or not critical to the success of the business. This process can follow a merger or acquisition as the new organization is shaped. Whilst it may appear easy on paper to merge an organization there is a good deal of work required before all systems, processes and staff can be integrated.

Many have realized that all out competition is not always in everyone's best interests and often will collaborate and make new strategic alliances. These alliances are designed to give mutual benefit to both parties and enable them to achieve something that would be difficult if they were to tackle it alone. These alliances are best formed with other companies who provide the same services, provide other services to similar groups of consumers or organizations whose service may be complimentary.

For example, the supermarkets that offer financial services do so probably to the same customer groups that a financial services provider might target; however these offerings might be in different geographical areas. The supermarkets do not necessarily offer their own products but can offer those of an established financial services provider. The products have been repackaged to look as if they are offered by the supermarket. This cuts down the set up costs for the supermarket and effectively makes them a retailer or re-seller, as they are for all their other products. Both sets of organizations win because the supermarket has been able to add a new product to its range and the financial services provider has been able to act as a wholesaler and will of course be making something out of the deal. The supermarket will also outsource the back office operations for these services to the financial services 'wholesaler', which can manage the operation more efficiently and effectively. As the supermarkets have highly skilled negotiators they will broker a deal is both attractive to them and to their customers. The contact centre is likely to be part of this collaborative strategy, however to the customer it will appear that they are staff operating from the supermarket. Another way of financial services providers acting as wholesalers is where organizations such as charities offer credit cards to members that enable them to raise additional funds and provide member benefits. The financial services organization gains additional clients and can be associated with organizations that do good works in society.

Competition is always going to be a feature of the financial services industry. As technology can be easily copied organizations within the financial services sector will have to rely on differentiation in customer service to attract and retain customers. For existing providers there has been a radical cultural change from the old ways of working to delivering a service through different channels to meet the changing demands of consumers.

1.6 Summary

The key issues affecting organizations that led to the contact centre concept were born out of a desire to reduce overhead costs and improve service to meet the consumers' changing lifestyles. Strategically there was a need to meet these changing demands profitably and in a way that would deliver real competitive advantage. The growth of new technology has enabled these demands to be met and contact centres are very attuned to staying ahead of the game in this respect. The decline of 'bricks and mortar' and the increase of 'clicks and mortar' have led to the restructuring of financial service providers and the emergence of new players in this market. Competition within the financial services sector will always ensure that rates of change increase rather than decrease.

Unit 2

How do contact centres meet the needs of stakeholders?

The aims of this unit are to enable you to:

- explain the rationale for contact centres to meet customer needs and maintain shareholder value;
- compare and contrast the developments in technology which have allowed contact centres to grow in number and sophistication;
- explain the effects of emerging trends in the external environment on contact centre delivery.

Unit 1 gave a strategic backdrop to why the contact centre as a delivery channel came about and the drivers that made this happen. This unit starts to look in more detail some of the operational issues that have affected the progress of contact centres as we know them today.

Contact centres all have a number of stakeholders. In section 1.1 we said that stakeholders are the different groups of people who have an interest in an organization and its activities. For contact centres this can be the organization's senior management, the centre management team, the employees at the contact centre, unions, suppliers, the local community, customers (existing, new and potential) and the shareholders of the organization. Each of these groups will have varying amounts of power to influence what happens at the centre and interest in doing so. For example the centre management will have high degrees of power and influence, whilst the local community will probably have a high degree of interest in the centre as a local employer, but will not have so much power to influence what goes on there.

Customers have a high degree of interest and they will be interested in how the contact centre can meet their needs efficiently and effectively. There are various ways this can be done and in this unit we will look at how technology can help meet customer needs and the needs of other stakeholder groups.

2.1 Standardization and specialization

In this unit we will look at how customer needs are met through the application of technology. Before technology can be applied to a process to improve customer service, there are certain criteria that have to be filled. Let's look at each of these in turn.

The process or flow of work has to be capable of being standardized. This means that there must be one simple way of undertaking the work to get the desired end result. It must be work that can be completed by an individual who can take sole responsibility for that work without having to refer to the rest of their team or line manager. Those tasks that require input from a number of team members, such as brainstorming ideas for a new sales initiative, do not lend themselves well to standardization, as this requires a high degree of creativity from a number of people and usually approval of budget from line managers.

Question

How does standardization benefit the customer?

Standardization benefits the customer, as they will experience a consistent service regardless of with whom they are dealing in the organization. This means any adviser in the team can deal with a query. Having to wait for the adviser they spoke to last time to become available therefore does not inconvenience the customer. If the process has been standardized well then the overall effect should be of an efficient and more effective service.

It means that the organization can make customers aware of exactly what level of service they can expect in their package and the service or product offered can be completely transparent. There will be no need for hidden charges or rules. All customers can be treated equally and this will lead to less complaints through special treatment given by one adviser and not another.

Many processes within financial services organizations were already standardized before the application of technology. This was because of the legal framework in which the industry operates. It is easy for local practices to spring up and this is where errors can be made and customer complaints arise. The application of technology to processes appeared attractive as it gave the opportunity to insist on the correct procedures being followed and ultimately saves cost and time. By applying technology to the processes it meant that everyone in the organization knows that there is a single way of doing things. In turn monitoring and control has been made much easier for management and problems can be spotted before they get out of control. An example of this is in the standardization of lending processes where losses due to individual managers' discretion have been reduced through credit scored lending applications.

The effect of standardization is that it gives very clear guidelines to individual's roles, which is important for any organization large or small. It gives minimum benchmarks for appraisal and training purposes, employees will know exactly at what levels they need to perform. This means that the right people can be recruited for these roles, which can be costly to the organization if this is not done.

With more 'self-service' delivery, standardization helps customers understand what information they need to give to get the answer they need. For example customers are now able to obtain loan quotations on a financial services provider's website. By having clear questions that need completing before the quote is given the customer knows what to do. This also is a way of making services more convenient for customers as they can undertake this sort of enquiry at their own time and at their own pace.

A further way of improving customer service following standardization is by specialization of employee roles into specific areas. This is because employees can be more effective if they can do one job really well, rather than several poorly.

Question

What are the benefits of specialization of employee roles?

The main benefit of specialization of employee roles is that customers' queries can be matched to the right advisers to give the correct information and to solve problems on the customer's first call. This means that, overall, customers are dealt with more quickly as their query is dealt with immediately and there is no need for them to make another contact taking up additional adviser time. The employee gains expertise and the team itself can become a centre of excellence for that area of work.

Individuals can choose those areas that interest them, so there are round pegs in round holes, eg some people prefer to be in a service role rather than a sales role. Specific training can be given and employees can feel some pride on their work. This then enables those that want to, to enhance their skills and knowledge by training for other roles, thus becoming multi-skilled. This would then allow them the opportunity for job rotation and progression.

From a management perspective it is easier to manage resources if individuals' skills are known and proven. This then enables managers to match the resource skill profile to customer demand patterns and any organizational customer initiatives.

Technology can be used to deliver standardization and specialization of roles. Automating work reduces monotonous tasks, for example the printing of cheque books used to be done at every branch by clerical staff. Nowadays the chequebooks are printed centrally and this enables employees to spend time with the customers rather than in routine back-office work. It can be seen that advisers have more time available for more complex and therefore more interesting issues. Technology allows processes to be followed without having to refer to manuals or line managers. The use of scripted delivery can help advisers learn roles more quickly and become confident in their skills.

Question

What is impact on levels of service given?

Standardization and specialization delivered through technology means that overall customer service can be improved, with queries resolved at customer's first contact. The total number of customer contacts can be reduced, thus having a positive impact on resourcing levels and adviser morale. Individuals should therefore be happier in their roles and be more upbeat when dealing with customers.

2.2 Cost base reduction

We have seen that one of the drivers for change and the emergence of the contact centre as a delivery channel, was the need to reduce costs whilst still maintaining good customer service. By standardizing and specializing processes and roles a financial services provider is able to use technology as part of the streamlining of the delivery of services and so reduce costs. Initially, many financial service providers did this by centralizing telephone contact to one place and taking out back office processing from the branch network, so reducing the need for branch premises. The strategy was to reduce the price per customer contact and, as already discussed in Unit 1, part of this was to remove the high overheads of a 'bricks and mortar' presence.

As mentioned in section 1.4 First Direct were the first successful organization to achieve both cost reduction and excellent customer service from this new way of working. Let's look at this in more detail in the example below.

Case study – First Direct

Midland Bank (now HSBC) in the late 1980s was worried that it was losing market share and knew that it could not claw this back using traditional methods. The bank did not want to acquire another organization to grow, so it undertook some research to see if it could understand why its market share was decreasing. Midland found that fewer and fewer people were going into branches on a regular basis, 51% of customers visited the branch as little as possible as they did they did not like queuing. 33% of people who did visit the branch said that had no personal contact when they got there. In addition the opening hours were inconvenient and 27% of people wanted to do more of their banking by telephone on a person-to-person basis.

Branches were therefore not well-regarded in terms of customer service, cost or profitability. Midland needed a solution that was cheaper but as effective as face-to-face service. It also wanted something that was radically different that would overcome the usual inertia of bank customers to change their account to a new provider. This required the new service to have both accessibility and innovation.

The result was to design a telephone-based service that had convenient opening hours, and that was simple and efficient. It also had to be sufficiently different so that consumers would not associate it with the big high street bank parent. So First Direct was born.

The 365 days-a-year, 24/7 service enabled customers to check account balances, hear details of recent transactions and pay utility bills without the need to write out and post cheques and to do all this with a person at the end of the phone. The First Direct team aimed at taking 100,000 customers in first 15 months and in fact gained around 500,000 and continued to grow by 10,000 per month.

They were able to keep costs down while maintaining high quality levels by (initially) having a single manufacturing centre with lots of distribution outlets – telephones. By having one centre there were one set of overheads with high quality people. It was backed up by Midland Bank branches and the bank's ATM network, which gave the new 'virtual' bank the infrastructure it needed to service customers' account transaction needs. Whilst First Direct grew quickly it was selective about who it opened accounts for (aiming for higher income earners). This meant that these customers would have more money to spend on financial services and be less likely to default on any borrowing arrangements. This meant that employees would spend less time chasing debts from problem account holders.

Going forward, First Direct tries hard to solve customer complaints and to manage the customer relationship to keep customers and acquire new ones through referrals. High levels of communication, both to internal and external customers, are key to this continued success. The organization fosters an open culture with hierarchy kept to a minimum and employee morale is considered important. The social aspects of work are emphasized to employees, through informal dress and non-work activities, so people do not feel like they are in a traditional 'bank' environment. In 2004 First Direct came in the top four companies for 'work and family', 'work/life balance' and the 'best service overall' in a *Sunday Times* survey. Furthermore, 76% of customers are either 'extremely' or 'very satisfied'. The message is that a happy workplace makes a happy customer.

The case study shows that First Direct was able to reduce costs and improve service and has continued to do so. As First Direct found in its first 15 months the accuracy of forecasting demand for new or even existing service can be problematic.

Question

What happens to the cost per transaction when the volume of contacts exceeds forecasts?

Unfortunately, high contact volumes push up the price per transaction, more advisers have to work overtime to clear backlogs and customers calls are dropped so causing increased volumes at a later time in the day as customers call back. Customers complain to advisers that they could not get through and advisers spend more time trying to calm customers rather than dealing with queries. Complaining customers exceed the number of first time customers with a query, so the call lengths get longer, increasing the costs and causing further pressure on contact volumes. The outcome is a downward spiral and lost service levels.

Therefore, organizations have to look at how the call volumes can be handled better to keep costs under control. For those simple account queries then there are automated systems such as Interactive Voice Response (IVR) systems that can perform tasks such as giving basic account information. New delivery channels such as interactive websites enable customers to access information themselves and input information to initiate payments and manage their accounts. This in turn reduces the cost per transaction particularly when the customers undertake the work themselves. It is estimated that 30% of customers use the Internet for their banking needs. Responding to e-mail requests is both cheaper and quicker for the customer and the organization. By automating transactions in this way financial services providers become more efficient and are able to deal with higher volumes of contacts. Higher volumes of contacts in turn mean more opportunities for sales. Higher volumes can mean that advisers capabilities become stretched so monitoring of the traffic needs followed carefully.

When an organization considers the merits of investing in a new delivery channel they must compare the set-up costs and the ongoing running costs, with the costs of the existing service. When setting up a new contact centre it must allow for growth because the cost of replacing infrastrucure to deal with greater contact volumes or the relocate the premises a few years later would not be acceptable.

2.3 Shareholder value

Shareholders buy shares in a company to invest their money and on which they expect a return, ie payment for lending money to the organization. This is similar to the way in which depositors expect to be paid interest for money they lodge with financial service providers. The attraction for shareholders is that the rates of growth, historically, have been better in the long term than deposits, which typically only increase by the amount of interest they are paid and are generally eroded by inflation.

Shareholders receive a share of the profits of the organization at the end of the organization's financial year. This payment is known as a dividend. If there are no or low profits the directors of the company are not obliged to pay anything to shareholders. If shareholders are lucky the value of the shares will appreciate, however this is dependent on a number of factors (eg confidence in the stock market) not just the performance of the company itself.

Organizations can 'go public', ie offer their shares to the open market, to raise additional finance to allow the company to expand and grow. Expanding their working capital in this way is unlike a bank loan, as they do not have to pay back set repayments each month linked to interest rates, or anything towards the capital amount. The arrangement is open-ended until such time the shareholder decides to sell their shares back on the open market.

Having gone 'public' these stock exchange quoted companies have the added pressure of the scrutiny of the city analysts, who influence the stock market and therefore share prices, and institutional investors, such as the pension funds, who want a good return for their customers.

'Shareholder value' became a useful tool to emphasize to those organizations, which were insufficiently focused on profit-making, cost-reduction and share price, particularly in difficult economic conditions, the need to improve share prices, where falls in these prices could lead to hostile takeover. Unfortunately it implies that the shareholders themselves have a high value, and therefore power, and can impose near impossible demands on top teams to produce perfect results every quarter. This has led to some short-term thinking by executives particularly where their permanency in the role was based on these quarterly results.

Some organizations have been accused of pursuing shareholder value above everything else – so alienating other stakeholders in the organization, such as employees and the wider community, and perhaps most importantly, the customer. The idea of making more profit does not necessarily inspire employees to greater efficiency, especially when those efficiencies may come at a cost to those delivering them.

We have already discussed that basic customer needs are for value for money and an efficient and effective service.

Question

What happens when the shareholder and customer needs are opposed?

Messages coming from an organization can be contradictory.

Marketing message: 'We are here to serve you as a valued customer'.
Investor message: 'We are here to make money, to give to you'.

When there is a tension between the needs of the customers and the needs of the shareholders there are some hard choices for the top team to make. They need to be fair to both parties in order to be successful and also take into consideration the other stakeholders that have an interest in the organization. They have obligations to treat customers well, employees fairly, and to treat the local community and environment in an even-handed way, none of which should be seen to be to the detriment of shareholder value. Shareholder value needs to be balanced by strong ethical values and corporate social responsibility. It is untrue to say therefore that the sole purpose of an organization is to make the shareholders wealthy.

Question

How do contact centres contribute to providing shareholder value?

Current thinking suggests that organizations should have a more holistic approach to shareholder value. Contact centres therefore are about more than providing an excellent service at the lowest possible unit cost to customers. Additional benefits that contact centre can bring in the long-term that will enhance shareholder value are:

- providing employment and prosperity to the local community in which the contact centre is situated and income to the surrounding area;
- using new ways of delivering service at lowest possible cost, embracing new technology to do this;
- providing employees with training and career development to maximise their potential;
- creating a positive work atmosphere, which is supportive of family friendly policies and work life balance; and
- involving unions in changes to working practices ensure changes made go smoothly with maximum of employee consultation.

Of course the contact centre is required to contribute to the organization's bottom line by generating income in a profitable way and this will in turn have a direct impact on the monetary worth of shareholder value.

2.3.1 *Summary*

Contact centres are required to meet customer needs and at the same time maintain shareholder value. By standardization of work processes and the specialization of employee roles the contact centre is able to apply more and more technology solutions to dealing with customer queries. These in turn reduce the cost base and increase the profitability of the centre. We must not lose sight, however, of the fact that there are many more stakeholders who have an interest in the contact centre and its activities. If the support of these other stakeholders is lost then the centre itself will cease to function to the full.

The next section of this unit is to consider the different types of telephony systems that have allowed contact centres to grow in number and sophistication.

2.4 Telephony systems

When considering the different systems available it is useful to understand some of the terminology used and the history of where it came from. This section of the text covers a number of these issues in overview so that you can understand the advantages and disadvantages of each.

Let us first deal with some terminology that you may have already encountered and which you may see again in this section.

- **Application infrastructure** – core technology of the voice switch (or phone system) that routes and manages calls. The voice switch is the device that connects callers to agents. Application logic is used to route and queue calls to advisers.
- **Network infrastructure** – underlying technology that physically transports the caller–adviser conversations. Until the past few years there has been only one choice for voice networking: circuit switching. This technology has been used for telephones for more than 100 years.
- **Packet switching** – uses high-bandwidth data networks to carry all forms of 'traffic' – data, voice and video. It includes 'Voice over Internet Protocol' (VoIP).

What an organization ultimately decides for the infrastructure within their own contact centre will depend upon what their business is and what legacy systems they already have.

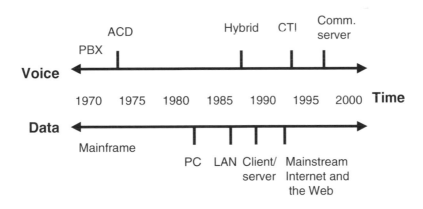

Figure 2. *Voice and data technology evolution*

Figure 2 shows the evolution of voice and data technology. We will now explore each of these in turn.

2.4.1 *Data technology*

Personal computer (PC)

Until the advent of the PC the world of data processing was dominated by mainframe and minicomputer. These systems came as packages and if you wanted to change supplier all the previous equipment had to be scrapped. For organizations this was a very costly exercise. PCs enabled purchasers to make different choices and to use different components to construct their systems. Industry-wide standards emerged which drove this 'interoperability' and, as buyers had more choice, the prices began to drop.

Local Area Network (LAN)

Standalone PCs were fine for a home user or sole workstation in an office, however commercial users wanted to be able to share information. Creation of the LAN enabled all the users to be joined together to share data resources.

Client/server computing

A server is a shared computer on a local area network that can be either as simple as one that handles printer requests or, more usually, very high powered. This means it can store and distribute data for a whole office as well as controlling access to voice mail, e-mail or faxes. These days' networks have multiple servers as the volumes of electronic traffic increase and the amount of stored data builds.

Internet

The Internet has accelerated a change in thinking about infrastructure. It has meant that many users can be connected easily and quickly from many geographic locations. It has also meant in the contact centre environment that adviser time is being taken up by non-telephony contacts. The volume of data traffic has overtaken the volumes of voice traffic.

2.4.2 *Voice technology*

Private Branch Exchange (PBX)

This is the core voice switch for most medium and large organizations. Many people just know it as the 'phone system'. A PBX is a specialized computer for managing all the phone connections in the office. Linked to this will be the automatic call distributor (ACD) software, which manages the calls within the contact centre.

The advantages of a PBX are that:

- one system can serve the whole organization;
- it can serve thousands of users;
- it has a high reliability;
- suppliers usually have a range of products and services, with support services; and
- it is a proven technology.

The disadvantages are that:

- the hardware and software are from one manufacturer so it makes it more difficult to use other providers, so can prove to be expensive; and
- the original technology was developed for voice rather than data and therefore not suitable for 'packet switching'.

Automatic Call Distributor (ACD)

The standalone ACD is a specialized voice switch that is best suited for the contact centre environment. Although similar to the PBX it only serves the contact centre telephone system. Often it will have completely different cabling to the rest of the organization.

The advantages of an ACD are that:

- it can serve hundreds or thousands of advisers;
- it has advanced features specially designed for contact centre use; and
- the sales and service support is dedicated to contact centre users.

The disadvantages are that:

- it creates a duplicate infrastructure to maintain alongside the PBX and this makes it costly; and
- the original technology was developed for voice rather than data and therefore not suitable for 'packet switching' and multi-media.

The hybrid

Customers began to demand more functionality and 'open architecture' (which means that the hardware of the contact centre can be made up of various different suppliers' equipment) from the PBX and ACD systems. To do this some suppliers moved some of the 'intelligence', eg capability for queuing, routing and adviser work states, to a server. This arrangement was called a 'hybrid'.

The advantages of a hybrid are that:

- it gives increased functionality and improved capabilities;
- extends the useful life of switching matrix or telephones;
- it is a more 'open' system; and
- it provides a path for multimedia queuing and routing.

The disadvantages are that:

- many still require all hardware and software to be purchased from the same supplier; and
- they may require dual administration on both the server and ACD/PBX.

Computer Telephony Integration (CTI)

This brings together the traditional telephone with client/server computing. The CTI can supplement or replace the existing switch (PBX or ACD) infrastructure. If used to supplement the switch then this means the data and software can be much more sophisticated. It will enable such facilities as screen pop-ups, predictive dialling and multi-media integration (eg e-mail, fax, web chat and web calls). If used to replace the ACD or PBX it doesn't dramatically change the functionality but changes where it resides and executes. This is sometimes known as 'dumbing down the switch'. Whilst the CTI appears very like a hybrid the CTI is much more sophisticated and also allows a variety of suppliers products to be used. This means that the architecture can be even more open.

The advantages of CTI are that:

- existing ACD/PBX hardware can be used;
- it is highly customizable;
- there is a choice of hardware servers;
- more software applications are available; and
- multi-media queuing and routing can be accommodated.

The disadvantages are that:

- there are some issues regarding scalability and reliability;

- may require dual administration of the PBX/ACD and the CTI server;
- the user may be locked into one supplier of software;
- support may be difficult if there are many suppliers and a high degree of customization; and
- the quality of the application is highly dependent on the voice-switch CTI link capabilities.

Communications server

With this option the telephone system runs on a standard PC system with standard operating systems such as NT, Linux or Unix. It is highly software orientated. The user can choose either a variety of components from their preferred suppliers or the supplier of the server provides a list of approved options/suppliers from which the user can chose. It provides a highly integrated capacity for voice-switch functions and contact centre application functionality for managing the centre.

The advantages of a communications server are that:

- it is highly integrated for routing and reporting;
- there is choice for hardware and software options;
- it has good application functionality for small and medium sized contact centres; and
- it is a good option for an organization that prefers to run its own IT support.

The disadvantages are that:

- reliability is highly dependent on the server, operating system, software and quality of its development;
- scalability can be limited if multi-site capabilities are required; and
- support and maintenances may be difficult because of multiple components and suppliers.

From the above we can see that the more reliance there is on software and PC systems the more sophisticated the functionality of the system becomes. The downside is that this can have an impact on the reliability and scale of the operation. The way in which contact centres have grown and will continue to grow will be based in the effectiveness of emerging technologies. The next section looks at another factor that has affected the growth of contact centres – centralization of operations.

2.5 Centralization of operations

Traditionally, a financial services organization consisted of a central or head office building (usually one for each of the separate parts of the business such as retail, corporate, life assurance, general insurance, mortgages and investments) with a number of regional offices in various parts of the country. There would then be a large number of local branches and offices within each region. The costs of supporting all these different premises in many different geographic locations would unsurprisingly be quite high. The traditional way of serving customers was on a face-to-face basis at these local branches and offices and needed a large number of staff to do it effectively. This increased the cost of service delivery.

Prior to the emergence of contact centres most companies have considered centralization of their operations in some way. Due to the limitations of communications and consequently the need for customers to be served on a face-to-face local basis, this option had previously proved to be problematic in the service industries.

Originally contact centres enabled the centralization of services through the use of the telephone as this medium developed as the main communication channel. This meant that customers did not have to visit their local branch personally. They could obtain a similar service over the telephone without having to go to the branch and queue to wait for a member of staff to be free to deal with them. To reduce the overheads caused by the branch network this telephone service could then be put onto one national site to deal with the requirements of customers across the whole country. This then reduced the need for branches and staff and the financial services providers reduced the number of local offices accordingly. The first time this was done (in the early 1990s) it did attract some negative press comment, however the need to remain competitive and provide customers with value for money was paramount.

Question

What are the benefits of centralizing contact centre services?

The benefits of a single centre site are:

- one site to maintain and operate rather than hundreds. This brings additional savings in security and improved employee facilities with newer and better offices and additional benefits such as a canteen and crèche;
- support services such as human resources, training and IT can be located within the premises so reducing the duplication of roles;
- less internal infrastructure required to support the advisers' contact centre software applications;
- less hardware systems where back-up or duplication is required;
- it can be situated in an area where there are sufficient suitable staff available to fill the adviser role. If the location is chosen well these staff can be employed at more favourable rates than in other, more expensive, parts of the country; and
- in some parts of the UK businesses are incentivized to start new operations through the availability of grants. This will make some areas more attractive in terms of greenfield contact centre sites.

Along with the benefits however there can be some disadvantages of a single centre site. These could be said to be:

- a single site means a single point of failure, which could be the building, power, telecommunications or systems. Under a disaster recovery situation the cost of recovering to a nearby site can be extremely expensive. This is probably the single biggest disadvantage;
- if the area is popular with other organizations that run contact centres then there may, in the long-term, be problems in recruiting the right number of new employees with the appropriate skills set or having to pay over the odds to recruit them. Once all the available staff in the location have been employed then obviously the supply of suitable people is severely limited and can cause issues with matching adviser resource to customer demand;
- if the centre becomes overloaded then there is no capacity to take extra calls. There may not be room to expand to create more adviser workstations;
- very large contact centres can be difficult to manage well and the levels of customer service could then be at risk; and
- customers may initially be worried that employees of the contact centre will not have the 'local' knowledge required to deal with their queries and could perceive the new service as 'impersonal'.

Contact centres became more popular as customers adopted the new delivery channel and customers identified a single point of contact and used it more. As the success of individual contact centres has grown, however, organizations have seen the need to increase the availability of this type of service. As we have said above, it is not really practical to keep increasing the size of one contact centre to accommodate the needs of all the organization's customers. This therefore means that the number of sites has to be increased. This leads again to a degree of 'decentralization', again with its own issues.

Question

What are the issues relating to several contact centre sites?

- Whilst there is the technology to make this possible, it means that the centres are reliant on technology and it has to be reliable for the centres to succeed. Having two or more sites does spread risk and reduce the impact of a total systems failure if one of the contact centres were to be offline.
- Overflow of demand can be catered for by re-routing calls to another centre within the organization with spare capacity so enabling high volumes to be coped with. Managing these resources against call volumes can in itself create new challenges.
- If the two centres are located a long way from each other then support roles will be duplicated, however if there are large numbers of employees within each centre this is probably not too much of an issue. The impact on operating costs should be weighed against maintaining service to customers.
- If centres are located within easy travelling distance employees may be able to swap roles across the centres to gain additional experience.

- Customers may perceive a differential in service from one centre to another and the organization has to ensure that this is not detrimental to the customer experience.
- In some instances, to achieve further cost reductions, organizations have sought to set up contact centres in foreign countries. At the time of writing the impact of decentralization to this degree is not yet clear.

2.5.1 *Summary*

In the last two sections we have looked at how developments in voice and data technology have allowed contact centres to grow in terms of their infrastructure and therefore their efficiency and effectiveness of dealing with larger and larger volumes of calls. Customers have adopted the use of contact centres as a means of interacting with their financial services provider and as these customers have identified this single point of contact, centres have grown and expanded organically. As one site cannot keep growing forever this means that again technology has enabled organizations to use multiple sites more effectively in order to match resources to call volumes. In doing so, however, they have to ensure that they do not encounter the same problems as the traditional branch networks of the past.

We will now move on to look at some to the emerging trends in the technology environment and their likely impact on contact centre delivery.

2.6 E-commerce and the use of websites

Customers are becoming more educated and more attuned to the need to be financially aware. As regulation means that customers have access to more and better information about financial products and services, their knowledge about such matters is improving. Customers also want to feel in control of their finances and are more willing to undertake routine transactions themselves. This means they will look for solutions to give them the information and control they desire. Use of the web and 'e-commerce' enables financial services providers to deliver both of these to customers.

E-commerce is an integrative concept, designed to draw together functions such as inter-organizational e-mail, directories, trading support systems, ordering and logistic support systems, management information and statistical support systems. Broadly, however, it can include any kind of business related transaction conducted with the assistance of electronic tools, even the telephone and fax. It usually relates to the exchange of information, such as when an individual looks for an item to purchase on the Internet and then also where money changes hands, for example where the individual purchases the item they have found.

For financial services providers it enables customers another route to self-serve and undertake a variety of transactions such as:

- account opening and changing account details;
- account balance enquiries and statement browsing, with the ability to print off information;
- interest rate enquiries;
- credit card authorizations;
- loan applications
- money transfers between accounts and bill payments; and
- ordering cheque books and statements.

This can be done at the customer's convenience, out of usual office hours if desired. It is also possible for customers to browse through product information, should they wish to take more complex products and services such as general insurance (typically car and household insurance) and stockbroking services for share dealing.

Think

> How does the information service offered by your contact centre differ from that offered by your organization's website?

Whilst being able to undertake all these tasks from a home PC makes sense from a customer perspective, there are also some good reasons why an organization would wish to invest in web self-service facilities for customers. The cost of a web enquiry or response is anywhere from one-tenth to one-third of the cost of a conventional inbound customer telephone contact. This therefore makes the web a very attractive channel for financial services providers who are looking to reduce their cost base and still deliver good customer service. The website is there to support the other means of communication and statistics show that customer to business call volumes have risen 30% since the advent of the Internet. Further research has shown that when a contact centre is coupled with a website, the two work better together than as discrete and separate channels.

This ability to self-serve has meant that customers can undertake their own 'banking' without the need to contact the organization and deal with an adviser. In some ways this is beneficial in reducing costs as explained, however it does reduce the opportunities an organization has to enable advisers to spot opportunities and cross-sell other products and services. This presents a dilemma for the organization, in that in an effort to reduce costs it could be missing prospective sales. The organization would need to be confident that customers who use the website regularly would be prepared to buy most services or obtain quotes using the website and were able to do so without further advice. With increased regulation and in particular financial services organizations' requirement to adhere to the 'know your customer' rules, this can become problematic. This also means that content for financial services providers' websites has to be thought through very carefully along with for the need for it to be refreshed regularly to attract the customer's attention. The ability to browse up-to-date information at the customer's leisure was something not always possible in the days of the traditional branch. The downside is that the customer might not find what they are looking for and go elsewhere, which on the Internet is very easy to do.

Personalizing the self-service experience is the next wave of sophistication for both web-based and other customer contact tools. Increasing levels of personalization are thought to improve customer loyalty and retain high value customers. For customers who self-serve over the Internet the future could be in an assisted service multi-media contact centre. In the contact centre of the future the customer who needs help could link into an adviser through a variety of means and deal with this adviser whilst using the organization's website at the same time.

2.7 Multi-channel delivery

We have seen that the financial services industry is dynamic and subject to a high degree of competition. The drive to improve customer acquisition and retention whilst containing costs means that financial services organizations need flexible, scaleable and reliable systems that deliver the right products and services, at the right time to the right customer. Banking, insurance and the products that were once the domain of the traditional building society are now being blended together, resulting in a broader range of services to a wider customer base. Any existing financial services providers are experiencing intensive pressures from new and existing competitors that threaten hitherto profitable areas of their business and market share. In this competitive environment technology plays a critical role in allowing differentiation of service that can enable an organization to stand out from the rest. While reinforcing their trusted and established role for commercial and retail customers, financial services providers are deploying next generation solutions that meet the rapidly changing needs of these customers.

We have seen in the preceding sections that multi-channel delivery, ie communicating with the customer in a variety of different ways so that each customer is able to reach the organization in a way that they prefer, is the most effective way of distributing products and services to customers. It should be the aim of the organization to ensure that whichever way they wish to interact with the organization, whether it is through the branch, by telephone or via the website, that the customer has a consistent and seamless experience.

However, the organization, in designing this customer 'experience', needs to be aware of the relative costs of providing each of these delivery channels. We have already established that 'bricks and mortar' was a highly expensive way of delivering service. Let us now look at the relative costs of some of the technology linked distribution channels.

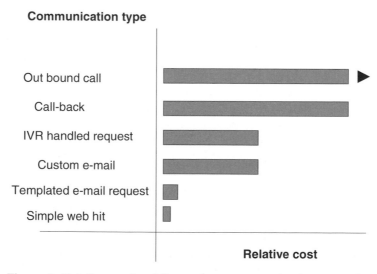

Figure 3. Relative costs of the various communication types for multi-channel delivery.

Figure 3 shows six different ways of customers communicating with the organization. You will see that a simple web hit is very cheap, as the costs of design and construction of the website are spread over thousands of visitors to that site. An e-mail request generated by a customer on a template from a standard screen specially designed on that site costs around three times more. Once a customer e-mails a request that needs a specialized response then that costs increases to ten times that original website hit.

When looking at the costs of contact centres a request handled by IVR Customer call-backs and other out bound calls can cost 20 times that much, possibly more. To that needs to be added to speed of response expected by customers and whether this can be achieved by the provider.

Question

For each of the communication types what speed of response do customers expect?

Customers tend to expect automated responses to happen immediately, for example they expect the website and the IVR system to give information straightaway. Less automated responses such as template e-mail responses and call back requests should either be the same day or within 24 hours. Generally the quicker the response expected by customers for non-automated communication the more expensive it becomes. You can see that if customers can be encouraged to use simple automated systems for routine tasks such as account transaction the cheaper and quicker it will become. This brings better value for the customer and improved profitability for the organization.

One of the pressing problems for contact centres with the desire to deliver multi-media distribution is that the advisers are also expected to work in all media, eg telephone, e-mail and letter. It may well be that advisers are not all multi-skilled in this way, those recruited for phone skills are not necessarily comfortable with using the written word and may not be happy being asked to do so without additional support. If, in the future, video becomes viable as a customer communication channel, will these same advisers feel at ease conversing with customers in this way?

From a customer perspective all the channels need to be integrated and managed cohesively. This means that regardless of which media they use customers feel that they are getting a consistent service from whichever way they chose to deal with the organization.

There are some other multi-media technology considerations. These are that:

- multiple sites for telephony will need multiple sites for other media too; the infrastructure has to be compatible;
- network security and reliability is paramount;
- forecasting, scheduling and reporting – media other than telephone doesn't necessarily fit in well with these tools – e-mails for example can be answered in seconds or can take hours depending on the nature of the enquiry;
- quality monitoring must be undertaken for other media and the means to do this must be possible; and
- a knowledge base must available to support advisers for the different media they are expected to work in.

The multi-media strategy needs to be considered in the overall corporate strategy, and whether the new distribution channels will bring the benefits required. Customers want choice and control. Telephone calls cannot be extinguished altogether – there is a need to interact with customers to discuss their problems and to find out how we can help them.

2.8 Other media choices

There are a plethora of different media developing in which organizations can enable interaction with customers. In this next section we will have a look at some of those that you may encounter; these are SMS text messaging, WAP phones and interactive digital TV. The aim of this section is for you to understand in outline what these different technologies are and how they may be used for customer contact.

2.8.1 *SMS text messaging*

SMS stands for 'Short Message Service'. It has been introduced as a useful and cost effective method of delivering information to customers. SMS is more commonly known as 'text' messaging which many of us are familiar with for sending messages to friends using a mobile phone. The service allows mobile phone users to send and receive text messages of up to 480 characters.

When a financial services provider uses the service to contact customers it will come from their message centre, or from the Internet, using a 'SMS gateway' website. If the customer's mobile phone is off or out of range, messages are stored in the mobile phone network and are delivered at the first available opportunity. This means that organizations can send information to customers advising them of new products or services, special deals and offers. For financial services providers it also means that customers can opt to receive mini-statements, bank balances and recent transaction information direct to their mobile phone. Customers can also choose to be forewarned that they are nearing a nil balance on their account, credit limit or overdraft limit. They can even be alerted to share price movements.

This technology is a very economical automated communication channel for the provider with very little capital outlay. For the customer there is generally no charge for the service and once set up, very little input from them is required.

2.8.2 *WAP phones*

WAP stand for 'Wireless Application Protocol'. Four companies – Motorola, Nokia, Ericsson and Unwired Plant, created it. It is a worldwide standard in mobile phone software that allows a mobile phone user to read Internet web pages on the screen of their mobile phone or hand-held electronic personal organizer. This means that users can have access to the Internet, see information, use services and send e-mails. This means effectively that WAP puts the Internet in your pocket so the potential benefits are great.

For customers of financial services providers this means that they can self-serve in the way that they would from a personal computer without having the constraints of being in a 'wired' environment. This means that customers can access account details wherever they are with the same levels of security and functionality.

A downside of using a mobile phone for this type of access is that the full graphics that we have become accustomed to with PC access to the Internet is not available on the small screen of a mobile phone. There are also some difficulties with navigation, as this has to be done with the phone keys rather than a PC mouse.

2.8.3 *Interactive digital TV (IDTV)*

This was first launched in the winter of 1999 by a combination of service providers including Sky, British Telecom, HSBC and Matsushita (a Japanese company). IDTV allows users to interact with their television set via a telephone line (land line rather than mobile) or a network TV cable connection. At launch interaction was fairly limited and in the main used for shopping channels and basic banking services. Today it offers users the opportunity to browse, shop, bank, send and receive e-mails and much more.

IDTV has opened up another route for communications between financial services providers and customers and potentially those customers that do not have a PC at home. Users can undertake similar functions they would be able to over the Internet from the comfort of their armchair whilst watching their favourite TV programme.

There are new technologies waiting in the wings. Some you may of heard of are 3G and GPRS. We will see EMS – Extended Messaging Service – that will allow text messages beyond the current 480-character limit and users will be able to send and receive simple sounds and animated graphics. MMS – Multi-media Service – will enable mobile phone users to send and receive messages with text, graphics, audio, video clips and photographs. You may already have a mobile phone that can do this.

2.8.4 *Summary*

In these last three sections we have seen how customers are embracing new technology to meet their demands for 24-hour access to information, flexibility and ease of access. We have seen how the different technologies can meet these demands in a variety of ways. The ability to self-serve appears to have become more important in recent years as customers' confidence grows. It is paramount for the organization to present these different delivery channels in a coherent way so that customers get a consistent service experience. What we must remember is that if a customer is having difficulty or wants advice and help, it is important that there is an adviser available at the end of a telephone to provide the human touch.

Unit 3

Contact centre information technology

The aim of this unit is to enable you to state the differences in contact centre technology infrastructure and the relationships between telephony and contact centre software.

We looked in overview in section 2.4 at the way that telephony systems for both voice and data processing had developed from the early 1970s to the present day. This unit is intended to give you a more detailed overview of the main systems in use today and how a contact centre manager would assess the suitability of these for use in their centre.

Information technology (IT) is an all-encompassing term given to the hardware and software of computer systems. As we will see in the next unit this is different from how the data collected by inputs to the system is managed.

In this unit we will focus on factors in the design of a contact centre and the main types of technology systems that are available. We will go on to look at the advantages and disadvantages of some of these systems and what factors are likely to be of interest to a centre manager when choosing technology solutions.

3.1 Factors in design

In this first section we will look at what factors affect the design of a contact centre infrastructure and the impact on the IT that would be used. This will be driven primarily by the organizational strategy and why the contact centre is required. It could be just to service existing customers in their day-to-day banking transaction requirements. Part of the centre operation may be to attract new customers and make sales and this will require different IT solutions. It may be that it is a complete new business with no customers and needs to allow for staged growth.

If this is the first contact centre the organization has set up it needs to consider carefully the profile of the customer base and the market that the organization is in. Many contact centres are set up to deliver a low-cost service to the majority of customers. This is because these organizations realise that their customers are cost-conscious and will decide on their provider on price. The contact centre makes a strategic contribution because it can deliver a decent service while containing costs. This type of contact centre should be capable of both inbound and outbound sales, delivering good customer service and be easily linked to other parts of the business for process efficiency. To achieve this it means that the way the contact centre is managed will focus on streamlined processes, and statistics, eg costs per contact, resource utilization and handling times.

Those contact centres that wish to provide high levels of sales and service will have a slightly different view on the focus of the centre. Systems will enable advisers to know their customers well and grow relationships. The customers wish to be treated as 'special' and are prepared to pay a little extra for this. The centre will have close relationships with other parts of the business for customer and product knowledge and support. The customer interaction will be focused on quality rather than statistics of the contact.

These two examples are of how the 'strategic fit' (see section 1.1) relates to contact centres.

Think

How does your contact centre relate to the 'strategic fit' of the organization?

Whatever the role of the contact centre in the strategic fit of the organization it will affect the type of technology used and we will look at this in section 3.3.

Initially the size of the contact centre and its potential for growth will be important. Is the site chosen going to be sufficiently large to allow for the projected call volumes? The infrastructure used will probably need to be capable of being networked to another centre in case the volume of business outgrows it. Is the existing site sufficiently large, is there room for growth and does the centre need to be capable of being networked to another centre? It may even need to be capable of being connected to a third party if some of the work is to be outsourced at a later date.

The location of the centre will be important, as we have mentioned in an earlier section. There needs to be sufficient local resources at the right cost and good communication links to enable employees to reach their place of work easily. In terms of the premises, some thought should be given to the levels of security required and who has access to what parts of the building. Obviously there will need to be restricted access to some parts where there is essential and highly valuable computer equipment such as the computer servers. With potentially large number of employees working on the premises out of usual office hours it may be the organization's policy to allow for additional employee benefits such as lounge areas, restaurant, crèche and even shops. This will be on top of usual facilities such as meeting and training rooms.

The type of business will affect the technology infrastructure chosen. If there are mainly, inbound calls only for customer service this will be different if it is sales environment where a large number of outbound calls are required. The amount of back office processing will also affect the technology infrastructure, as will the number of administration users who do not require connection to customers such as human resources, training, resourcing and IT support. Many contact centres are dedicated to the organization's own customers, however some do act on behalf of third parties to whom services are outsourced. An example of this would be the services undertaken by a financial services provider on behalf a retailer of financial products such as one of the supermarkets.

In addition to levels of inbound and outbound contact, the types of contact, eg telephone, e-mail, post, fax and web-based services will affect the information technology chosen. How the advisers and their team leaders are to manage each of these contacts will require consideration. Linked to this is the need for reports and management information. There will be a requirement to assess the quantity and quality of the contacts and link this into the management of each individual's performance and appraisal. The management information must be capable of giving an overview of the activity of the entire operation to allow resource forecasting and planning. More coverage of this topic is given in Unit 4.

Whoever designs the contact centre infrastructure needs to have a close eye on what happens in the event of a systems failure and how such a disaster can be recovered. This could be through the loss of external power or computer failure. The amount of resilience required to overcome such catastrophes can be built in at the start as is sometimes known as systems 'redundancy'. Building in extra redundancy (or capacity) could be by providing on-site electricity generators for essential power, having a dual processor for the computer or in the event of a total shutdown of the centre, where the operation could be relocated to quickly.

Obviously none of the above comes cheaply. In the planning stage the returns on investment and impact on customer service will need to be examined closely. Setting up a contact centre is a major investment for any organization. The contact centre must be seen as a long-term venture that supports, and is integrated with, other parts of the organization.

3.2 Main types of system and what they do

In section 2.4 we had an overview of the various voice and data systems that evolved since the 1970s to the present day. Here we are going to take a more indepth look at those systems and some others that you may encounter. This will then enable us, in later sections of this unit, to understand their various advantages and disadvantages when applied to different contact centre scenarios.

3.2.1 *Private Branch Exchange (PBX)*

This is a smaller variety of the organization's larger telephone system or 'switch'. The main difference is that besides the size, it resides in your contact centre and serves you and your customers. This means that advisers have the ability to dial out themselves without having to go through an office switchboard. The PBX manages the flow and routing of incoming and outgoing calls.

A PBX allows the contact centre to build its own infrastructure and therefore has a degree of flexibility. It is possible to connect electronic phones to this system making it easy to identify calls and transfer calls within the centre. Good reliability with more open architecture and the possibility to connect software to a PBX, which makes the functionality simulate that of a larger system, makes the PBX a good choice for the smaller contact centre. It is also possible to have a PBX with the features of an ACD, so it is possible to try out the idea of an ACD before committing to the expenditure of installing one in the contact centre.

3.2.2 *Automatic Call Distributor (ACD)*

An ACD answers a call and puts the call in a pre-specified order in a line of waiting calls. In the most basic terms it ensures that the first call to arrive is the first call to be answered. It can also deliver calls to advisers in a pre-specified order, to those that have been in idle the longest or to the next agent that becomes free. There is the capability to specify many possible variations in the order of calls and advisers depending on their skills levels and other variables.

The other main feature is that it can provide detailed reports on many aspects of the call transaction, including for example how many calls were connected to the system, how many calls reached an adviser, how long the longest call waited for an adviser, the average call length and so forth.

Originally ACDs were highly specialized telephone switches that could serve over 100 workstations. These days the ACD can be linked to a PC, a PBX (this arrangement is known as a known as a hybrid), or a server; they can integrate with other contact centre technologies and nationwide networks of ACDs that can act as a single switch.

There is no technology more suited to routing a large number of inbound calls to a large number of advisers than an ACD. Whilst it is both fast and efficient at routing calls it won't necessarily suit every business application. On a per seat basis it is more expensive than a PBX although more sophisticated in terms of processing power and special features. Many ACDs lack the functionality of a basic telephone system so making an outbound call can be complicated.

Figure 4 shows the process used by an ACD to manage an incoming call. Whilst dealing with the call it will collect real time information about such things as the total number of calls handled, which calls are have been directed to which hunt groups and the status of individual advisers. Much of this information can be displayed on the centre's wallboard or on the adviser's workstation phone or screen. It also enables team managers to listen to calls, if necessary either join in or take over the call if the adviser starts to have difficulties. These are just a few of the main features of an ACD we will look at some more of the reporting functionality in the next Unit.

3.2.3 *Computer Telephone Integration (CTI)*

This is a term for connecting a computer, whether this is a single workstation or server on a LAN, to a telephone switch where the computer issues the switch commands to route calls. Basically, calls come into the centre carrying a user identification. The switch hears the calling number and sends it to the computer. The computer checks its records and sends back the switch instructions on what to do with the call. Therefore the switch follows orders.

ACD answers call and plays greeting
announcement

Announcement continues that agents are
busy and through an interface with the
reporting system says how long that wait will be

Asks for customer's account number and
Personal Identification Number which can be fed
to the adviser through a 'screen pop' when the call
is taken

Announcement offers option of solving problem
obtaining information through IVR system

The ACD may then route the customer query to
the correct adviser group based a on a variety of
criteria than can be pre-selected by the contact
centre administration

The agent handles the call and statistical
information about the call is collected and stored
by the ACD

Figure 4: *The process used by an ACD to manage an incoming call.*

This might be to send the call to a specialized adviser (skills-based routing) or to send the call to the adviser that dealt with it last time (data directed routing).

The term covers many technologies not just telephony; interactive voice processing, voice mail, automated attendant, voice recognition, fax, video conferencing and predictive dialling to name a few. This is why it has become more popular with multi-media contact centres.

It also enables a wider variety of software to be used that can be fully integrated with the centre infrastructure. An example of this would be a customer relationship management system.

3.2.4 *Outbound calling*

Where outbound calling is a feature of the contact centre's activity there are various ways in which this can be done.

- **Manual dialling** – using the keyboard or keypad to place calls.
- **Screen dialling** – dialling from an object on the adviser's screen (eg name, number) and receiving an indication of the call progress on screen.
- **Pre-view dialling** – a list of customers to be called is maintained by the computer system and the call list or data relating to the next person is presented to the adviser. The adviser then initiates the call by a simple indication (eg by clicking on an on-screen 'go' button) or by using screen or manual dialling.
- **Power dialling** – the power dialling controller has a list of numbers to be called, a number of outgoing telephone lines and a group of advisers. It launches as many telephone calls as it possibly can and, as soon as an answer is detected on a particular line, attempts to connect the call to an adviser. If no adviser is free it drops the answered call and launches another. Note that this type of dialler (and the predictive dialler) detects and removes all calls that are not answered or completed for any reason. It will also detect fax machines and attempt to detect answering machines, ensuring where possible that advisers do not waste their time on these devices.
- **Progressive dialling** – at least one adviser must be free before a call is launched. The controller detects that an adviser is free, selects the next call to be made and makes it. The call will be either connected directly to the free adviser or it will be connected when an answer is detected, as in power dialling.
- **Predictive dialling** – this is similar to power dialling however it is far more subtle. It is a compromise between power and progressive dialling in its effect. Here, rather than launching a mass of telephone calls regardless of the adviser availability as the power dialler does, the controller uses a 'pacing algorithm' such that the rate of launch is based upon the probability of an adviser being free. The predicative dialler tries to predict the precise time to launch a call such that an adviser will be free within a specified period of the call being answered eg one second.

3.2.5 *Voice processing*

Voice processing is the term used to cover all the technologies that allow you to record, retrieve and manipulate the spoken word, especially over telephone lines or a telephone switch. Some of the different technologies are outlined in more detail below:

- **Voice response unit** – this term is commonly used to mean the automated voice system run by the ACD that welcomes the customer before they get to an adviser. It may offer the customer information, eg a railway timetable announcement, weather report or account balance. It may also contain a routing function that allows the customer to choose which help desk they need to speak to.

- **Interactive Voice Response (IVR)** – this is effectively a telephone interface to a computer system and is important in a CTI context. It allows the customer to enter information into the system either through a telephone keypad or the spoken word. The customer will then receive information from the system through a recorded voice or synthesized voice. By accessing information via the telephone this enables customers to access information from anywhere in the world. It also reduces the need for advisers to be answering monotonous, simple queries. Used as a front-end for an ACD an IVR system can ask questions such as 'what is your account number?' that help in routing and enable more intelligent and informed call processing by either advisers or automated systems. IVR can fill wait time with valuable activities that make the adviser's job easier through information popped onto the screen when the customer gets connected to them.

- **Voice messaging systems** – this is the recording, storing, playing and distributing of phone messages and takes the benefits of voicemail beyond the immediate office to any phone destination selected. The basic functions of the voice mail application are the so-called RSPFR functions. These letters stand for the functions required to:
  - **R**ecord messages
  - **S**end the message, to one, or a number of other mail-boxes
  - **P**lay messages
  - **F**orward them to someone else
  - **R**eply directly to the sender.

3.2.6 *Adviser support systems*

There are also a great number of adviser support systems that appear on the adviser's workstation PC. These can be in the form of call scripts, Intranet knowledge bases, customer relationship management systems, customer information systems, product/process information systems and so forth. These are usually highly customized to each organization and therefore difficult to explain in general terms.

Think

> How many different support systems do advisers in your contact centre have access to from their workstation PC?

It is worth mentioning that whatever systems are run, these have to be easy and quick to use. They also have to be easy to integrate into existing legacy and future programmes.

3.3 Advantages and disadvantages of various systems

You will have seen from the last section there is a wide variety of systems available and if you were to then compare them supplier by supplier the choice would become even greater. In this section we will look at which systems are best from the perspective of the size of the contact centre, its strategic fit and a number of other factors that should be taken into consideration.

3.3.1 *Contact centre size*

The switching system is the one largest of the parts capital expenditure for a new contact centre and if the incorrect switching solution is chosen this can create issues once the centre goes live. A small contact centre of say less than 30 adviser workstations would probably have a PBX based ACD system or a PC based small ACD system. It is unlikely that there would be a standalone ACD because of the expense, however if growth was planned it may be installed. A medium-sized centre of say 30–100 adviser workstations is more likely to have a standalone ACD, as this keeps the traffic away from the rest of the organization's telephone system. The cost is also more affordable at this level of usage. In a large contact centre of 150-plus adviser workstations an ACD is fundamental to managing most of the cost of the centre. It is unlikely that any of the other options would be suitable at this size because of their limited functionality by comparison.

The plans for the centre's growth must be considered closely before any firm decisions are made. It is important that this growth is not under estimated as this can obviously affect what equipment is bought. It is key that, whatever supplier is chosen, they understand the business and its potential growth and whether the system being sold will actually fulfil the organization's requirements.

3.3.2 *Strategic fit*

Depending on the strategic role of the contact centre in the organization it will mean that some systems will be better than others. The following table shows examples of which systems fit best to low-cost leader and best service and sales strategies.

Low-cost leader strategy	Best service and sales strategy
• Multi-skilled agents who take in-bound and out-bound calls • Web-based access for customers which reduces call volumes • IVR which reduces adviser time • CTI which can produce screen pops to reduce adviser time on calls • Predictive dialler for outbound call efficiency • Reporting system linked to a financial management system • Robust workforce management and scheduling system • Easy integration to other parts of the business such as processing • Customer access not 24-hour	• Comprehensive CTI-enabled CRM • CTI data-directed routing • Skills based routing to specialized advisers • Various applications with scripts, call flows and work flows • 24/7 customer access • Easy integration to other parts of the business such as branch staff, face-to-face advisers and processing

You will see that the low-cost centre has far more automated features that reduce calls and less sophisticated routing options. There is also a high focus on adviser performance through call statistics collected via the workforce management system.

3.3.3 *Other factors*

There are some other factors that will affect any system's suitability. The first of these is an 'open architecture'. Many of the new systems available on the market are more open than ever before and these are extremely useful for those organizations that intend to develop their own sophisticated call routing or voice applications. It will mean that the ACD can integrate with various external computer systems or databases without the need to develop bespoke software. This also adds to the system's flexibility.

The system administrator will wish to re-configure and re-route calls quickly and easily to cope with call volumes. They will do this via their PC by dragging and dropping icons around their screen. These icons on the PC monitor are called a 'graphical user-interface'. In the early days this was done through complex computer code, which required many hours of training to understand fully. You can see that the ease at which this can be done now is a great advantage.

When looking at some of the disadvantages then cost will be raised as an issue. The more sophisticated the system, and the more open it is, the greater the cost. Large amounts of money are also spent on developing software to be flexible and stable under load. This part of a business case for a contact centre will always come under close scrutiny and so should be researched thoroughly with potential technology suppliers.

Support for all the various systems is obviously required and the more technology suppliers there are, the more complex this becomes. In addition, where there are linked contact centres in different geographic locations supporting them can become problematical. Where centres are based overseas local support may not be available and bringing in personnel to do this work adds to the cost of maintenance.

Finally there is the issue of depreciation on the capital cost and the fact that technology dates quickly. In some cases this can mean that it is in fact cheaper to re-new a system completely rather than try to keep upgrading it.

3.4 Criteria of choice for the contact centre manager

When choosing the best systems for the contact centre the centre manager will have a number of areas to consider.

Question

What will affect the choice a contact centre manager will make over the purchase of new systems?

We said at the beginning of this unit that the centre manager will need to understand fully the centre's role in the organization and how this links to the centre's own objectives. This relates to the type of business the centre is in and who its customers are. Added to this is the nature of the activity undertaken at the centre such as inbound or outbound calls, back office processing and what customer media is being used, eg website, e-mail, telephone and post.

It may be that the centre is a new standalone centre, however it may be a new centre that is linked to existing centres, which will provide parameters for choice, as the systems used need to be compatible. Inter-operability of systems with other parts of business and other systems in the centre will be essential. This is where having an open architecture is advantageous and good service agreements with the suppliers to ensure the system is maintained well. Whatever system is chosen, it needs to be reliable under high volumes and have sufficient redundancy in case of failure. The ability to customize the system is high on the agenda as this enables the centre to continue to meet the demands of customers and employees, without having to undergo a major systems overhaul.

Easy to use monitoring equipment for voice and data recording enables team managers to track adviser performance on both a real time and historical basis. This will allow them to benchmark performance across the centre. The information can be used to inform training and development plans and for individual reward purposes. This sort of management information is clearly important, as is the ability to manipulate and present data in a way that is easily understood by all.

The adviser facing systems, ie the 'front end' should be simple, easy to train, easy to use and quick. It needs to enable advisers to get their average call handling time down rather than hinder them by being overly complex. There can be some useful additions such as a training mode that can be customized, a knowledge base, and links to the organization's Intranet (for facilities such as FAQs, self-help site, and an employee chat page) and internal processes, such as holiday requests. The centre manager may be interested in peripherals such as wallboards and probably a PC suite for training purposes. This all adds to the cost and balance between budget and facilities needs to be struck.

A strategy for technology is therefore required that links into business objectives. Problems can arise where the benefits from business cases are not realized, and the cost outweighs the benefits for both advisers and customers. It is important that the technology group and business group have common goals and priorities and work together to achieve the desired vision. It is imperative that the technology is sufficiently flexible, scalable and adaptable to meets needs of the business as it grows. Just because a centre has the best equipment doesn't necessarily mean that competitive advantage and cost reductions will automatically be achieved. The centre manager needs to remember that people make it happen.

3.5 Summary

In this unit we have considered some of the main IT systems used in contact centres. There are many factors to be considered and a wide number of choices from suppliers in the hardware and software market place. Due to the high cost of technology solutions this investment needs to be considered carefully to ensure it delivers the desired results and creates a good customer experience rather than eroding the service that customers have previously received.

Unit 4

Management information

The aim of this unit is to enable you to explain the growth of management information systems in a contact centre environment.

In the last unit we looked at how technology supports the running of a contact centre in terms of physically dealing with contacts. In this unit we are going to look at how technology can help manage primarily the employees within the contact centre environment. How it can be used to help manage the customer relationship will be covered more fully in later units. In terms of the employees management information systems can be said to:

'improve the performance of people in organizations through the use of information technology.' (Sprague and McNurlin.)

The ultimate objective is performance improvement, which is based on the achievement of objectives. The focus is the people who make up the organization, in this case the contact centre advisers. The resource to measure and track this improvement is IT systems, such as the ACD and workforce management software.

In this unit we will explore the role of information in the decision-making process and why it is important. We will look at the different types of information available and how it can be stored and retrieved. In the final part of this unit we will look at databases and how they can help the team or centre manager manage their team.

4.1 Information and decision-making

Information is one of the key elements in the design, operation and performance of any contact centre. The more information that can be collected and analysed from customers, the ACD and in-house systems, the more accurate forecasting of calls, market or sales trends will be. Ultimately it should be easier to manage the effects of these trends. The management information system (MIS) in itself does not make the decision for the user. The users have to apply their knowledge, experience and judgement to reach conclusions and take action.

Question

When managing the performance of the centre what sort of objectives will centre managers be interested in?

The sorts of objectives that contact centre managers will be interested in when managing the performance of the centre will probably be as follows.

Quantitative measures, where information can be collected via IT systems:

- the revenue generated from the calls and deviation from these objectives;
- individual adviser performance;
- the service levels achieved for incoming calls; and
- network and system component performance (eg IVR, ACD queuing and routing functions).

Qualitative measures, where information is collected via customer feedback and adviser observation:

- the quality of the customer experience and whether this generates goodwill;
- the accuracy of the information given to the customer; and
- the skill, attitude and morale of the advisers when dealing with customers.

Getting further into the detail there will be a number of questions that will concern that centre managers.

- How many calls/e-mails are being handled, when and who by?
- How long is the average call length and is it possible to reduce this or improve the quality?
- How many customers hang up before talking with an adviser?

- How long are customers willing to wait for an adviser or a response to an e-mail?
- How are advisers spending their time when they are not taking calls or replying to e-mails?
- Is the workload being distributed fairly among adviser queues?
- Do we need more adviser positions to cope with call volumes and maintain service levels?
- How have the effects of 'seasonality' affected volumes over the past year?

There will clearly be many more questions that the centre manager will have depending on the type of business they are in, however this gives you a flavour of what their concerns will be and the type of information they require.

With this information the centre manager will be able to make important decisions regarding resourcing of the centre. This means how many full time employee positions are required, how many advisers should be on which shift and what their skill requirements will need to be to meet daily call patterns. In addition these patterns differ across the year, ie the seasonality, which needs to be factored in. The gaps between what resource is available and what resource is required will give information on training needs, along with individual call and e-mail monitoring. The centre manager will wish to ensure that overall service levels are reached and that a high percentage of calls are answered and dealt with first time. He/she will want to ensure that there are the right resources at the right cost to do this.

Imagine now that the organization's head office wants to run a campaign that will lead to more sales of a particular product or service. The centre manager and their team will need to forecast what adviser resource is required to meet expected customer demand. Based on historic data from previous campaigns it may be possible to estimate what the volumes will be based on the number of customers multiplied by their 'contact propensity'. Contact propensity means the probability of a customer calling or e-mailing the centre, which can be given a numerical value. For example the organization could estimate that 20% of customers will contact the centre about a new loan with a lower interest rate following TV advertising. Factored into this would be whether that contact was by telephone or e-mail. Having an indication of what customer response will be to the campaign enables the centre to plan and cope with demand without causing undue stress on either technology systems or advisers.

Unfortunately volume forecasting and scheduling to meet this volume is not an exact science and sometimes reality does not go according to plan.

There are a large number of variables such as product launches at short notice, product changes, price changes and other seasonal factors, such as the weather, that can affect customer contact levels. It is also likely that when they do contact if it is about bad news that will increase average call handling times and good news will reduce it. These sorts of issues will need to be considered.

The offer of contact 24 hours per day, seven days a week to suit customer requirements unfortunately encourages customers to behave at their whim and with a degree of unpredictability. Whilst calls can be forecasted with a fair degree of certainty within a 30-minute interval, exactly where within that 30 minutes is much harder to determine. Associated with that is the randomness of agent availability, as interactions with customers may be short or long, as well as a variety of different wrap up tasks which take variable amounts of time. Putting more resources in doesn't always mean that more calls will be dealt with.

Much of the thinking around the concepts of random call arrival, staffing and service levels was done as long ago as 1917 by a Danish telecommunications engineer named AK Erlang. He devised a set of tables that have been incorporated into computer programmes that allow managers to estimate staffing and numbers of lines required given the volume and duration of calls, and the service level desired. There are two types of Erlang formulas you may encounter, Erlang B, which is used where the traffic is random and there is no queuing and Erlang C, which is used where traffic is random and there is queuing. Both assume that callers will wait indefinitely to get through and that no calls are blocked. These are not really valid assumptions for the modern contact centre, although when the trunking is correctly sized and there is low abandon rate it can get quite close. Furthermore Erlang assumes that each agent is multi-skilled, which doesn't really meet the needs of a specialized multi-skilled environment.

Whichever workforce management software system the centre uses to manipulate forecasting and scheduling information, the aim should always be to reduce operating costs while increasing service to the caller. Failure to adequately service the incoming customer contacts can lead to losses of:

- revenue;
- customer loyalty;
- the expenses involved in initially recruiting that customer; and
- the expenses involved of carrying the call only to fail to provide the service.

Obviously over-staffing is equally as undesirable as under-staffing, unless of course there is some reason why the service delivered in customers and their reason for calling far outweighs the cost to the organization.

4.2 Types and sources of information

Management information systems are now as important as the switching platforms themselves. Information on the volume of calls and performance of advisers is important as we have seen in the last section, but there is other data, that is equally important, particularly to financial services organizations.

Question

What other types of information are there?

4.2.1 *Customer information*

To financial services providers customer information is key. Information supplied by the customer will be for example:

- name; first names, surname and title;
- date of birth;
- address;
- telephone numbers;
- e-mail address;
- occupation; and
- standing order and direct debit details.

Advisers will need to have easy access to this information so that they can fulfil customer requirements.

There will then be the information collected by the organization about the way in which the customer deals with them, eg:

- account profiles, for example for a current account whether there is an overdraft limit and whether the customer stays within it;

- pre-set limits on accounts based on account history so that advisers can authorize overdrafts without having to refer to a line-manager;
- products the customer has been offered and bought (past and present);
- details of previous contacts, so the customer's history with the organization can be tracked and possible future sales identified.

The organization can then run central reports such as those detailing out of order accounts that require action or customers with large credit balances that can be contacted with a view to moving the money to a better interest bearing account.

4.2.2 *Internal information*

There will be other internal information that the organization will want to collate to assist in customer service and sales. These could be Intranet-based knowledge bases for advisers to refer to so that up-to-date features and benefits of products and services can be accessed easily. When speaking to customers an adviser can use screen flows to take them through various processes such as stopping a cheque or ordering a credit card. This enables advisers to take details as the customer speaks, fulfilling the need to obtain all the required information in one go.

Internal records regarding employee information will be required, eg human resource information for each adviser, their name, address, date of birth, employment record, salary details, pension entitlement and so forth. Their appraisal records are likely to be kept electronically by their line manager along with training plans. The scheduling programme will contain details of advisers' holidays, sick leave, training courses requested, overtime and links to the payroll department to ensure that every month advisers receive the correct wage payments

You will see that there is a vast amount of electronic information all held on a variety of databases, with different people having access. There will also be different levels of authorization depending on what the activity is, eg customer third-party payments will be at higher level than amending addresses. A smooth interface between each set of data is important to avoid manual re-keying, which can lead to errors.

In customer facing roles it is important that advisers record accurate information given by customers. It is equally important that internal information is recorded correctly, for instance by the human resources department about employees. To ensure that the performance of the centre and so its advisers can be tracked properly, then it is essential that advisers key the correct reason codes when changing work states. Reason codes are numeric codes that advisers are required to enter when they change to auxiliary work or after call work mode or when they log out. They indicate the reason for the change in state. This tracking and reporting allows managers to understand more fully ways in which advisers are spending their time. This then enables better use of resources and scheduling. Every time a call arrives, gets routed, queues or is placed on hold, it creates a message. Every time an adviser logs in, changes work states, hangs up or transfers a call, it creates a message to the ACD. So a lot of data is being created. This data is written to a database and accessed through a reporting application such as SQL.

The key statistics that come out of the ACD reports give numbers of:

- calls offered;
- calls handled;
- calls abandoned;
- service level achieved;
- talk time plus wrap up time giving overall average handling time;
- average speed of answer; and
- trunk utilization.

This means that real-time statistics can be displayed on wallboards and telephone terminals. Advisers can watch their progress and make decisions based on contact centre conditions, eg requesting a call back to a customer. Team managers can also monitor the progress of each of their advisers, adviser groups, applications and trunk groups.

Managing the contract centre well is not just about statistics. An adviser may well be given these daily, certainly weekly and monthly by their line-manager and will probably form the part of the basis of their ongoing appraisal and training. Too much focus on statistics can lead to reduction in quality as advisers rush to finish calls and move on to the next one. This then leads to re-work and ultimately higher volumes. Any statistical monitoring has to be backed up with observation and coaching to ensure that the quality of calls is also maintained.

4.3 Use of management information

In this section we will look at some of the ways information is used to manage the contact centre. There are four steps information goes through before it can be considered.

1. Data gathering
2. Calculations
3. Report generation
4. Presentation

The management style and use of this information is critical to the orderly management and long-term operation of the centre. It is also key to ensuring that the goals of the centre are met as outlined in section 4.1.

As we have seen in 4.2 there is a rich resource of information that needs to be arranged in such as way that it is accessible to user. The information is therefore arranged in databases and manipulated by a computer programme – a database management system. Figure 5. shows a simple database structure for customer records. Records can be added for each customer. The number of fields can be virtually unlimited, however, it is usual to set restrictions to make it easier to manage. Searches can then be made across the database by using one of the fields as a reference point and search across that reference point with a known piece of information. For example if you knew a customer's name, using the customer name field as a reference point you could search though the names until a match was found. When a match is found then all the information on that line or 'record' will be associated with that name. If there is no match then an error message will be sent back such as 'item not found'.

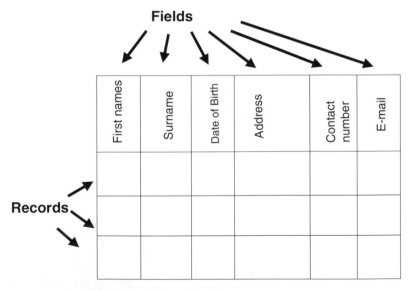

Figure 5: *Structure of a simple customer database*

The example in Figure 5 is of a customer database. In terms of managing the contact centre, an operational database for a contact centre would contain different information and we have considered this in section 4.2. There may be some calculations that are undertaken by the database management system before a report is generated to give weekly or monthly (depending on the period the report is required for) averages.

Think

How is the weekly performance report of statistics for each adviser in your contact centre presented?

The reports that team managers will use can be in a table of figures, perhaps showing the whole team and how the individual has fared against the team average. It might be in a graph format, either pie or bar charts, which when used can be easier to identify trends. The team manager will look for conformance and adherence. 'Conformance' means – have you done what you should have done and 'adherence' – have you done it when you should have done it. The team manager will be looking to give praise and recognition to those that have achieved or exceeded their objectives. To those that haven't they may wish to discuss with the individual the reason and to explore what support they need. The outcome for both parties should be to try to improve performance to ensure that service levels are meet and the customer experience is good.

For managing the centre as a whole, there is the need to have the right number of advisers at the right time to answer an accurately forecasted volume of calls at the service level required. As we have seen this is not an exact science, however, there are some good software programmes that can enable the centre management to have a good attempt. These are known as 'workforce management systems' and will deal with such areas as forecasting, scheduling and tracking.

Forecasting will need to be undertaken and can be done by breaking the day into 30-minute segments. For each segment there will be different call volumes on which there will be historic data. It will need to be adjusted by such factors as seasonal variations and any local inputs, eg one off sporting events which customers are likely to be watching on TV. The average handling times that can be affected by such things as organizational marketing campaigns or whether there are currently high levels of complaints about an issue outside the control of the contact centre, eg centrally initiated price

Forecasting

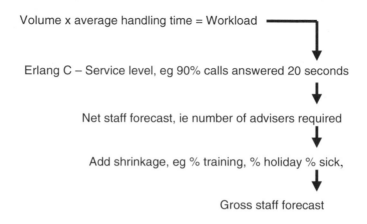

Volume x average handling time = Workload

Erlang C – Service level, eg 90% calls answered 20 seconds

Net staff forecast, ie number of advisers required

Add shrinkage, eg % training, % holiday % sick,

Gross staff forecast

Figure 6: *Forecasting process*

rises. By multiplying volume by average handling time together a workload for each segment per day can be calculated.

By putting the workload figure through the Erlang C tables for whichever service level is desired, in our example 90% of calls answered within 20 seconds, the net staff forecast can be calculated. By adding shrinkage, ie an allowance for people on training, on holiday or off sick, the gross staff requirement can be arrived at. The gross staff figure shows how many full time employee positions are required to meet service levels at any given segment of the day allowing for all the other activities that advisers have to undertake. This means that schedules can then be drawn for each adviser linking their shift to the forecast. There may still need to be some fine-tuning based on past experience, however the aim is to reduce schedule inefficiency.

Once the schedules are implemented then the individual adviser performance is tracked against the schedule. If an adviser is sick, it is therefore essential that their team manager knows about this as soon as possible as it will impact on the schedule and forecast for that day and rescheduling activity will need to take place. Advisers should ensure that their scheduled activities match their actual activities as closely as possible. This is known as real time adherence and the success of the centre depends upon it.

At this point it is worth remembering that adviser performance is not just based on statistics. The quality of the adviser call is just as important and as we have said this has to be monitored through line manager observation and coaching. Advisers need to be given clear guidelines on what the standards are for their behaviour and what competencies they are required to display. This can be easily linked to their other appraisal objectives and they can be rewarded for displaying the desired skills and knowledge. The line-manager team can create electronic databases for this sort of information that can be used to support agent growth and development. Just because the information is qualitative, it doesn't mean that it cannot be recorded and retrieved electronically.

4.4 Summary

We have looked at how management information systems can assist the management team achieve the goals of the contact centre in both quantative and qualitative terms. There is vast amount of information flowing into the centre, both from customers and staff. This unit has enabled us to look at what internal information there is and how it is used. Information is important in the decision-making process for the centre as it forms the basis of how the centre is resourced. The forecasting and scheduling activities will only be as good as the data input into the system and it is vital that this is accurate and up-to-date as possible. The quality aspects of the service to customers can be addressed if the systems are in place to do so.

Unit 5

Marketing in a contact centre environment

The aim of this unit is to enable you to describe the concept of marketing and how it relates to contact centres.

The majority of organizations want to grow and increase their business. We saw in Unit 1 that one way of increasing market share is to acquire a competitor and so take over their customer base. If this is not possible or desirable then the business must grow 'organically', in other words by the organization's own efforts. To do this successfully they will need to invest in some form of marketing activity that enables them to gain more customers to increase market share or sell more products and services to existing customers.

Marketing is not just another name for selling, although selling does form part of the marketing activity. As we shall see marketing is both a business 'function' (many organizations have departments that look after central marketing activity) and it is also a business 'philosophy'. This means that it permeates all aspects of the business so making the customer the focus of what everyone does. It is important that concern and responsibility for marketing reaches all parts of the organization, even those parts that are not customer facing. Let us now look at what marketing is.

5.1 What is marketing?

There are many different definitions for marketing and it can mean different things to different people. Kotler, a leading American marketer, said that marketing is: 'human activity directed at satisfying needs and wants through exchange processes'. This definition shows the requirement for work and formal activity, to give what people want or need from a product or service. 'Exchange' implies that there is a transaction of some sort taking place, usually products or services in exchange for financial remuneration.

The Chartered Institute of Marketing in the UK proposes that the definition of marketing is:'the management process responsible for identifying, anticipating and satisfying customer requirements profitably'. This definition suggests that customers are at the heart of marketing activity and businesses ignore this at their peril.

Think

> How have the products that you buy, or stores you visit or choices that you make been shaped by the forces of marketing in some way?

The marketing process is central to the business performance of organizations of all sizes because it addresses the most important aspect of the competitive marketplace, ie by identifying, anticipating and satisfying customer requirements profitably. The marketing function of an organization will study market forces and factors and the development of the organization's position to optimize its benefit from them. The management process of marketing is therefore about:

- getting the right product or service to the customer;
- at the right price;
- in the right place;
- at the right time.

How an organization plans to do this is represented in a simplified format by Figure 7, the marketing planning process. We said in section 1.1 that organizations have strategic objectives that are communicated to customers and employees. These tend to be quite high level and without precise measures, eg 'to be the best retail bank in the world'. The external business environment is ever changing and these statements need to be reviewed and amended over time.

One way for organizations to review their strategic position is via a SWOT analysis. SWOT stands for the following.

- **S** – strengths of the organization. This could include special unique products, a first class level of service or the best employees. These are positive aspects to help the organization grow.

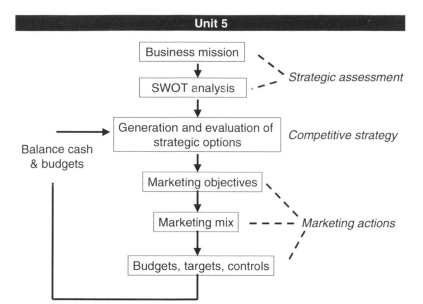

Figure 7: *The marketing planning process*

- **W** – weaknesses of the organization. This could include poor management skills or products that are uncompetitive. These are negative aspects that need to be addressed.
- **O** – opportunities outside the organization. This could include identified gaps in the market place through the advent of new technology. These are positive aspects that should be taken advantage of.
- **T** – external threats to the organization. This could include aggressive competitors or new legislation that would impact on sales and service delivery. These are negative aspects that should be watched or overcome.

Strengths and weaknesses relate to factors inside the organization and opportunities and threats relate to factors that are outside of the organization and to a degree outside of its control. It could be that the organization will wish to use external research to provide them with this information as well as internally collated feedback from customers.

Having collected all the research together the analysis of the SWOT factors will enable the organization to compare strengths with weaknesses and match this to opportunities and threats. This helps the organization make strategic decisions about the state of the market they are in, where in the market they want to go and how they are going to get there. This will be translated in marketing plans to assist the business in achieving their operational plans. These will link directly to the strategic aims.

The scope of marketing is very broad as it encompasses the whole organization and the way in which it meets the customer needs. One way to understand this broad scope is via the 'marketing mix' or the seven 'P's. These are outlined below.

5.1.1 *Product*

As we have said customers need to be happy with the product or service in order to buy it. It has to be of the right quality and at the right price. It is important that external research is undertaken before the product or service is launched to ensure that there is a market for it. The case study about First Direct in section 2.2 demonstrated the type of research that was done before the telephone-banking concept was launched. Once a product or service has been launched it is important that there is a system in place to constantly check whether it is still meeting customer needs.

5.1.2 *Price*

The right price means that not only do customers find the price acceptable but it also needs to give a profit and be competitive. Being competitive doesn't always mean being the cheapest. Value can be added to products or services by giving add-ons that costs the organization little but the customer values greatly. An example of this could be a free binder to keep bank statements in when an account is opened.

5.1.3 *Promotion*

This is how the organization communicates with its customers. This can be in the form of brochures, leaflets, websites, letters, advertising and personal selling. In whatever format it must grab the customer's attention, be appealing and be clear so that customers can identify which product is right for them. In the financial services industry organizations are given clear guidelines about what they can and cannot say in marketing literature so that customers are not misled.

5.1.4 *Place*

This is where customer buys the product or service and it is the means that the organization has of making it available to customers at their convenience. This is where the contact centre has come into its own as a place; it is a delivery channel enabling this customer convenience. CIM customer surveys have shown that the performance of an organization's delivery, or 'place' is one of the top criteria when a customer chooses a supplier.

5.1.5 *People*

People are a very important part of the marketing mix and any person coming into contact with customers can have an impact on customer satisfaction. In a contact centre environment the adviser is inseparable from the organization and its products and services from the customer's perspective. This means that they must be appropriately trained, well-motivated and the right type of person for a customer-facing role.

5.1.6 *Process*

As we have seen many of the processes in contact centres are automated and the behaviour of people, both customers and advisers, in using these processes are crucial to customer satisfaction. Issues such as queuing times, whether customers are kept informed, whether advisers are helpful and if the processes are making the service more efficient, will need to be considered in part of the marketing mix.

5.1.7 *Physical evidence*

The service from a contact centre cannot be sampled before it is bought as can be done with a physical product. This means that potential customers may perceive a greater risk when deciding whether to use a service. If possible physical evidence such as brochures or websites provided to potential customers to enable see what the service might be. This will enable them to provide a positive perception before they buy.

A well thought out organizational business plan should include the seven Ps of the marketing mix. These should link into budgets, targets and controls and cascade through the organization to departmental plans, team plans and individual plans in the form of appraisal objectives. Individuals can then see how their involvement will contribute to the success of the organization and therefore themselves.

5.2 Different marketing strategies

Different organizations will have a different approach to their marketing strategy and how they interpret the seven Ps we have discussed above. Clearly there will be a balance that needs to be struck between the needs of the organization and its customers and what the competition can do to meet those needs more closely and profitably. Doing this effectively can be difficult and Figure 8 shows how focusing too much or too little on one can impact on the organization.

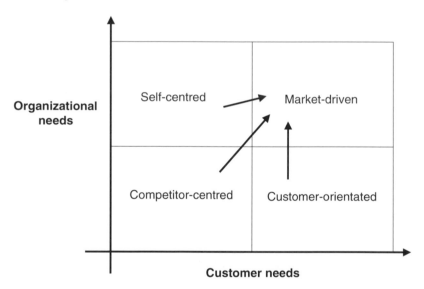

Figure 8: *Different marketing strategies*

In practice one of four scenarios can occur.

- Competitor-centred – this type of organization focuses neither on itself or its customers and is focused entirely on its competitors. Ultimately its success is limited because it does not look to the external environment to try to anticipate customer needs or to the internal environment to assess its own strengths and weaknesses.

- Self-centred – these types of organizations do not focus on the external environment of customers and competitors sufficiently and constantly look to internal measures as the benchmark of success. These types of organizations do not compare their results with other peer group organizations or ask customers for feedback on their products or services. This means that over time products or services cease to meet customers changing requirements so that competitors can win these customers over with a better offering.

- Customer-orientated – here much attention is paid to the needs of customers, which in a sense is good, however, the danger is that customer needs are met to the detriment of the organization. In a worst case scenario the customer could be receiving a Rolls Royce service, however the costs to the organization may be more than it receives in income, leading to losses and eventual closure of the business.

- Market-driven – this is where all organizations should aspire to be, hence the arrows in Figure 8. This means that the needs of the organization and of the customer are equally important. This also means that the organization remains competitive within the marketplace.

Think

> Where would you put is your organization on the grid in Figure 8?

An organization needs to determine its strategy and where its position is in the marketplace. It can then undertake marketing activities to achieve competitive advantage. There are a number of ways that this positioning and competitive advantage can be achieved.

- **Low–cost leader** – this type of organization offers a low cost product or service to a large number of people. An example of this could be some of the low-cost supermarkets that only offer own brand products at low prices.

- **Differentiator** – this product or service is sufficiently different for many people to want it and they will be prepared to pay a higher price for this than other similar products. For purchasers of DVDs, this could be the next Harry Potter film carrying a premium price. To be an effective strategy over the long-term this product or service must be difficult to copy.

- **Focus** – this is where the target market is much smaller and the focus can either be on cost or differentiation. Examples of this are services to the first-time buyer (ie on the cost of the mortgage and special income multipliers) or wealthy investors (premium service provided). Another example of this is the best service and sales strategy described in earlier units.

An organization needs to be clear which strategy it is pursuing as the danger of not doing so leads being 'stuck in the middle'. This means that the organization tries to be all things to all people and therefore satisfies only a few customers some of the time.

5.3 Marketing trends

The biggest impact on marketing in recent years has been the Internet. It has provided new ways for organizations to reach their customers and for customers to find out information they need quickly and easily. Many organizations however small will have a website and this enables them to make up-to-date product or service details accessible at the fraction of the cost of printed brochures and postage.

This development has allowed organizations to re-personalize the way in which they deal with customers. Customers can be sent relevant information about a purchase via a website within minutes to their desktop PC via e-mail and they can view their 'shopping basket' at any time. Another spin-off from websites and this type of personalization, has been delivery to the customer's door. Supermarkets have taken advantage of this by re-introducing home delivery, which used to be the domain of the local shopkeeper. For a nominal fee the customer can sit at home and order groceries from the supermarket's website and receive them at home without ever having to go out. This sort of service would have been thought of as too costly to provide five years ago. With improved physical distribution and delivery services many organizations have taken advantage of this from books, flowers, chocolates, clothes even holidays and hotels in foreign countries. The list is endless.

A way of personalizing contact centre contacts is by telephone network identification data. In the case of inbound calls, call type identity is being increasingly enhanced by the use of a variety of telephony features. The first of these is expanded DNIS (Dialled Number Identification Service) which directs customers to a specific group of advisers depending on what telephone number they have called. So for example, customers who wish to call about a query on a new account would use a different number for queries than a customer who wanted to make a query on an on existing account. Another way is by calling party number or ANI (Automatic Number Identification). This enables advisers to see on their screen the number of the person who is calling them and thereby receives the customer's information on screen at the same time. Finally voice response technology to request more specific identification (eg account number) from frequent callers enables customer data to pop up on screen at the same time as the call is put through. All these methods add to an enhanced customer experience.

This voice response technology has facilitated customer relationship management (CRM) systems, linking the front end of the customer interaction with the large data resources of the back office operation. From a customer perspective this means that the adviser has information on the customer and their past history when they take the call. It results in better and shorter calls that generate more revenue and are more refined and purposeful. We will look at CRM in more detail in Unit 7.

Customers are taking up technological innovations more quickly than in the past. For example DVDs are replacing videos and have been taken up twice as quickly than when CDs replaced vinyl records. Most households have a mobile phone and approximately half the households in the UK have a PC that connects to the Internet. This means that e-mail contact will become more important in the next few years and organizations must find ways of enabling customers to deal with them using this media. The down side of the increase in the use of e-mail is the increase in Spam, effectively junk mail, which plagues e-mail users. Added to this is the security of websites, particularly where purchases are being made or customers are accessing personal information using passwords. To be effective and retain customer's trust this security must be first-rate, as any breaches would cause damage to the customers and to the reputation of the provider.

Brands continue to be powerful and effective in influencing consumers to buy. There are many ways that brands have developed. Personalities and celebrities become brands and are able to endorse other products. An example of this is the Beckhams who generate the their own media interest and appear in the newspapers. As they are very well-known they are in demand to promote other products such as sportswear or fashion. Consumers will buy a product, not necessarily because of the product quality, price or design, but because they associate with the celebrity who advertises it and aspire to their lifestyle. In effect the promotion of the product or service becomes the most important of the seven Ps. One organization may have several brands, which meet the needs of different sectors of the market place. So for example HSBC have the HSBC branch network for customers that prefer face-to-face contact and First Direct for those that prefer telephone contact. The two brands are quite distinct, with marketing of the image managed separately. At the time of writing (April 2004), TV advertising of HSBC group has highlighted the global reach of the organization whilst operating on a local basis to suit the needs of that country.

Globalization is another challenge for organizations and how they manage marketing activities. As many industries are going through a period of consolidation, technology makes it possible to communicate easily with colleagues in other countries. For HSBC the challenge is to manage global organizations locally, whilst still having consistency of brand, so that a traveller going from one country to the next would recognize the organization wherever they went. Several years ago McDonalds opened a number of fast food outlets in France, which raised outcry from some of the local people. To adapt to the local market the product range had to be modified to suit, for example the introduction of the 'Croque McDo'. Some product have to have their names changed to make the product consistent across the world, eg the 'Marathon' chocolate bar had its name changed to 'Snickers'. Outsourcing to foreign countries adds to the increase in globalization and the matter of managing part of the customer service process remotely is raised.

Consumers are becoming increasingly concerned about where products are from and how they are sourced, eg genetically modified crops, child labour. Organizations also have to ensure that they behave in a socially responsible way to treat all stakeholders fairly and by taking their part in protecting society in terms of world security and terrorist threat. Financial services providers play a key role in this by following 'know your customer rules' and being vigilant for money laundering. Having a strong code of ethics and publicly contributing to good causes can also be an effective marketing tool as customers who perceive charitable works and identify with the espoused ethics of the organization will want to support it.

5.4 Marketing in the contact centre

In this section we will look at how marketing works in the contact centre environment however to do this we must first look at the difference between marketing products and services. Many organizations sell physical products that the consumer can see, touch and feel. They can gain experience before they buy. Financial service providers sell services and it is not possible for the consumer to do any of these things before they buy.

Question

How are services different from products?

Marketing experts acknowledge that marketing a service is more difficult than marketing a product. This is because services have a number of unique features that need to be considered.

- **Intangibility** – the service cannot be touched or viewed, so it is difficult for consumers to tell in advance what they are going to get. This in itself makes evaluating the service quality difficult and potential customers will look for other visible indicators of quality, most generally based on the experience they have in interacting with the company adviser.
- **Inseparability of production and consumption** – the service is being produced at the same time that the customer is receiving it, eg speaking to an adviser about taking out a loan. This means that the people involved are one of the most important factors when marketing services. Both the organization and the customer must interact for the service to occur and therefore both parties become part of the service provided. As such, the actual quality of services may vary depending on who provides the service, when and how.
- **Perishibility** – this means that unused service capacity cannot be stored for future use. For example spare seats on an aeroplane cannot be transferred to the next flight and quiet times during the day cannot be stored to serve customers during peak periods. This means that service organizations may encounter problems if demand fluctuates and service opportunities are missed. Strategies must be developed to ensure that demand is at a constant flow or that service can be matched to fluctuating demand. This is one of the biggest challenges for contact centres.
- **Heterogeneity (or variability)** – services involve people and people are all different. There is a strong possibility that the same enquiry would be answered slightly differently by different people or even differently by the same person at different times. To overcome this

and minimize the differences in performance through training, standard setting and quality assurance.

Organizations try to overcome some of the difficulties in delivering service by ensuring that the physical features of the service such as the website, documentation and advertising indicate the quality of the service. This will be supported if the people who deliver the service, ie the advisers, are responsive, reliable, courteous and competent. If the documentation is tatty, or the website is slow, disorganized and difficult to navigate with broken links and poor functionality, then customers may assume that the services provided will be equally inferior.

In contact centres the problem of perishibility is sometimes overcome by pricing strategies such as offering freephone numbers to highlight commitment to customer service and therefore not charging customers for holding. The value of the freephone service is quickly lost if the wait is too long. The other option is to install a queuing system. The queue content can be matched to the customer profile and the reason for calling by differentiating between prospects, first time callers, ordinary and premium customers and all differentiating between the call content; service or sales enquiry. For example first-time callers could be informed of the website and its functionality, whilst existing customers could be informed of new services offered by the Internet. Callers could be told information that is beneficial or interesting to their own circumstances and at the same time promote the brand in a manner consistent with the corporate image.

Call queues need not be seen as a necessary evil in which the organization ignores customer service and therefore its brand image. The quality of the queuing system is an integral part of the customer contact strategy. It requires a significant amount of resource to examine how it can be developed to subsequently improve some of the key performance measurements such as abandoned and answered rates.

Question

What can you do to address the queuing issue?

There are a number of actions that can be undertaken to address the queuing issue:

- measure the number of customers who have to wait and how long they wait and whether this wait is acceptable;
- examine the variance and maximum wait time, not just the average;
- estimate how many of your customers are calling back and how many never call again;
- consider how much business is lost through abandoned calls and how important your abandon rate is to senior management;
- quantify the effects the queue has on brand image and the qualitative factors of the call: whether long wait times lead to customer complaints that advisers spend too much time addressing;
- hold workshops with customer service advisers, customers, marketing and management to try to identify and measure the qualitative factors; and
- understand the tools and techniques currently available to assist with the queuing message.

For general day-to-day servicing of customer needs, contact centres need a basic level of call handling capability. When a contact centre wants to run a marketing campaign it is vital that it has the ability to generate and handle the volumes it expects and to ensure that it is well-managed. If the contact centre management do not plan for the campaign in a thorough way this can lead to an excess of demand over capability and the failure of the campaign. So before the campaign is launched the contact centre management should agree with the marketing team what goals and objectives are to be achieved for the centre. This will be as well as any additional business gained.

Question

What contact centre objectives should be put in place prior to running a marketing campaign?

The following contact centre objectives should be considered before running a marketing campaign.

- **Grade of service** – how long will the calling customer have to wait before being handled by the contact centre?
- **Talk time** – what is the estimated average length of call expected to be? How will this impact on existing resourcing and service levels?
- **Expanding the caller's tolerance for delay** – various methods can be used to encourage callers to wait, how is this to be done for this campaign?
- **Adviser wrap-up time** – what activities are advisers expected to do after a call relating to the campaign and what impact will this have?
- **Call load** – is there any part of the campaign that can be handled by an automated service so reducing expected call loads.

To ensure that customers are satisfied and remain satisfied with the service provided, the optimum for a contact centre to maintain the brand image should be to:

- decrease waiting time for customers;
- decrease transaction times;
- handle large volumes of calls when required;
- continue to improve the quality of the call handling; and
- increase network reliability and contact centre availability.

5.5 Marketing and the customer

Getting the right balance between demand for service, and supply of resource to provide it, is imperative to the marketing of any service. This will ensure that the organization has the capacity to attract new customers and retain existing ones. Furthermore to ensure that the business is successful it is important that the organization maintains good relationships with all its stakeholders, not just its customers.

As employees are part of the stakeholder group, internal marketing is required to ensure that employees treating each other as customers. In a contact centre setting this is ensuring that back office processors and customer facing advisers work as a team to provide the best possible service to the external customer. Everyone in the organization has to communicate well and not lose sight of the purpose of the organization – to serve the customer. Internal communication can be problematic when people work shifts and don't often meet face-to-face, however this can be overcome with some thought and innovation.

The quality of the 'buyer–seller' interaction is key in whatever setting this happens to be. The service has to be technically correct, ie any information given about the customer's account or service they wish to use and also be delivered in a way that satisfies the customer for example polite, responsive and empathetic to the customers needs. This will enable a provider to differentiate themselves for other competitors and the management of this service quality will be important. When a customer perceives the service, ie what they experience, to be better than the service they expected, then they are more likely to use it again. On the other hand many customers become aggrieved when the service they receive does not live up to their expectations. This means that service providers must identify what customer expectations are concerning the service to be delivered. If they want to remain competitive then they need to deliver it as far as possible within their budget parameters. Due to the nature of service (as we have seen in section 5.4) this identification of customer expectations may be difficult to do precisely. Whatever is decided upon as the service offering, this must be clearly communicated to the contact centre advisers and their back office support and their performance standards and objectives aligned to this.

A customer will tell others about an experience they have had with the organization and this will reinforce people's perceptions. Unfortunately it is more likely that a customer will relate a bad news story to more people than a good news story. This means that if a number of customers are having a similar poor experience then bad news will travel very quickly. Unfortunately not all customers will complain to the organization, they just quietly close their account and move their business elsewhere. The contact centre can help with the marketing effort by listening to customers' complaints however onerous this may feel, take appropriate action and advise senior management of the issues with possible solutions. Customers are less loyal than they used to be and will quickly move their business away if they are getting a better deal and there is nothing else in the relationship for them. This is particularly true of the mortgage market in which customers see a better interest rate with another lender. When the opportunity arises they will move their mortgage account elsewhere and for mortgage providers customer retention is a big issue. Trying to retain customers with penalty tie-in periods following special interest rate deals tends to annoy existing customers, as they see new customers being able to access interest rate deals they can not. Mortgage providers need to find other ways of building customer loyalty, such as providing excellent current account facilities so a borrower is more inclined to stay with them through that aspect of the relationship.

Keeping in close contact with customers enables organizations to observe and make improvements to their products and service to better satisfy their needs. This can be by running customer satisfaction surveys, holding customer focus groups or conducting independent research with the general public. In the marketing equation customers are extremely important. Organizations that pay little attention to the feedback from customers are damaging their ability to engender customer loyalty so compromising their future income and profits. Customers are likely to spend more money with an organization that values them and their business and recommend them to their friends. They are also less likely to be irritated by price increases if they feel the service they receive is value for money.

The role of adviser as interface between organization and customer is therefore essential and should be performed to the highest possible standard. For the time that customer is interacting with adviser, the adviser is the organization, and as such carries a great responsibility in representing it.

5.6 Summary

Marketing is about satisfying customer needs in a way that is profitable to the organization. To be effective it should be undertaken by all employees of the organization, as the organization exists to meet its customers' needs. Marketing activity starts with analysis of the organization and its fit with the external environment. The seven 'P's give the scope of the marketing mix and are all the factors that need to be considered when marketing products and services. Organizations will use different marketing strategies and position their products/services so that competitive advantage can be achieved. Changes in marketing trends have shown that organizations cannot stand still and have to be constantly searching for new opportunities so as not to be left behind.

The unique features of services make marketing in the contact centre environment different to that in retail outlets and other face-to-face delivery channels. Issues such as queuing, where the customer cannot see the length of the queue, need to be considered carefully in the contact centre context. Getting the right balance between demand for service and supply of resource to provide it is imperative to the marketing of service and this is the top of any contact centre agenda.

Unit 6

Marketing tactics

The aim of this unit is to enable you to explain the ideas of customer markets, segmentation and buyer behaviour.

This unit is about how the organization uses customer information to market and sell products and services. Some of the activities described here will be undertaken by the marketing function and some by advisers in their dealings with customers. It is important to remember that how well advisers interact and match services to customer needs is vital to make the most of any central marketing activity.

We will cover customer markets and how those markets can be segmented and how this can be used to reach customers with services that are appropriate for them. We will then look at buyer behaviour and how contact centre advisers can use this to their advantage. Understanding buyer behaviour is key to managing the customer relationship from both an organizational and adviser perspective.

6.1 Defining a customer market

Question

What does the term 'market' mean?

The term 'market' refers to the place where buyers and sellers meet. It will usually be defined as 'all the possible buyers'. There are so many potential buyers some organizations will not want to target all buyers, as this is just too costly to manage. Many potential buyers do not purchase immediately and in many cases they won't purchase until some years after a product or service has been launched. An example of this would be when a new family car is launched. Many people do not feel that they need a new car immediately and will wait until they think they have had value for money from their existing car before trading in their existing model.

The organization must therefore decide how it wishes to define the market. A market can be defined narrowly, eg all females between the ages of 25–30 or very broadly, eg all families with school age children. The organization will define the parameters based on their market research. When considering this the organization needs to bear in mind the resources available to execute its intended marketing strategy. By defining a broad market the organization will need a large operational base to back this up. Another effect of defining a broad market is that the number of competitors will potentially increase, as a larger number of providers try to attract a share of the market. Conversely by defining the market narrowly the opposite will be true.

Forecasting demand, as we have seen in Unit 3, is not always as easy as it may at first seem. Where new products or services are concerned if they are completely unknown to the customer then this adds to the complication.

Question

What are the issues with forecasting demand for new products or services?

There are a number of difficult questions to be answered when forecasting demand.

- How can the number of customers be predicted and targeted for a product or service that is unknown?
- If the product or service is launched into an already established market, how will the competition react?
- What is the probability of other competitors copying the product or service and joining the market and what impact will that have?

- Customer preferences change, how will the launch of a new product or service affect the dynamics of that market?
- How stable will demand be once the product or service has been launched?

Most organizations will realize that their product/service will not appeal to everyone in the market. Instead they must identify 'segments' of the market in which customers will find the product/service suitable for their needs. The organization then needs to decide which 'market-coverage' strategy it will use; this means how many segments of the market will be covered and how to identify the best ones.

There are three types of market-coverage strategy available to organizations. Undifferentiated, differentiated and concentrated as shown in Figure 9.

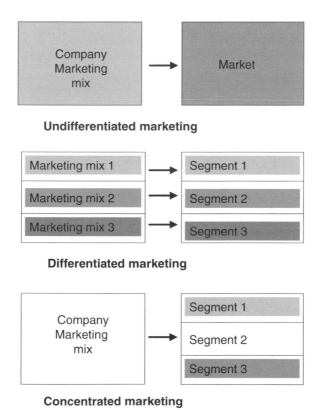

Figure 9: *Market-coverage strategies (from Kotler and Armstrong)*

When an organization selects an 'undifferentiated' approach it ignores the difference between market segments and approaches the whole market with just one offering. This approach is based on common customer needs rather than differentiated customer needs. It is intended to appeal to the largest number of customers. It can be beneficial and cost – effective as the target audience is wide. The downside to this type of marketing is that is can be difficult to produce a product or service that will actually satisfy a large number of people. It is therefore better suited to commodity products that are similar across all makes and brands (such as tinned tomatoes).

Choosing a 'differentiated' marketing strategy allows an organization to target a product or service in several segments with separate special features for each. This type of marketing approach has become more popular and organizations have seen the benefit from higher levels of sales than in the undifferentiated approach. The disadvantage is the increase in cost, as the promotion has to be adjusted to fit the different segments, eg different advertising campaigns and product features. An example here might be of a snack manufacturer producing different versions of crisps to appeal to different segments, eg hand-made crisps for dinner parties, novelty shapes for children and crisps with dips for young adults. All the same basic product but altered slightly to fit the segment.

A 'concentrated' marketing strategy can be useful to an organization with limited resources. Concentrating on this type of approach enables the organization to focus most of its resources on pursuing a large share of one particular segment of the market. This therefore enables organizations to gain a strong market position in the segment of their choice and provides a way forward for the future. It gains greater knowledge of its part of the market and can respond to changes within it. It has danger for the organization in that it is 'putting all it eggs in one basket' and therefore can be vulnerable if a large competitor moves in or the market changes very suddenly. An example might be of an exclusive fashion designer who specializes in evening gowns for high-profile celebrities.

6.2 Segmentation

As we mentioned in the last section 'market segmentation' is the division of a totally mixed market of buyers into groups with relatively similar needs. Every market can de divided into groups of people with similar characteristics. Segmentation is important as customers have unique needs and wants. Organizations thinking about introducing a marketing strategy should first understand the difference between a need and a want.

A need is the basic force that motivates a person to do something. The basic human need is a state of felt deprivation, the physical need for food and clothing for instance, a social need to belong and an individual's need for knowledge and self-expression. These are needs that require satisfying. A want is the form that a human need takes as shaped by culture and an individual's personality. So it can be said that a person wants an object that will satisfy their needs. For example everyone needs some kind of liquid to quench their thirst; this is a basic human need. Rather than satisfy this with water people have learned to drink coke or lemonade, a want created by their social environment and advertising.

Question

What factors can be used to segment customer markets?

There are three main segmentation variables, based on the following.

- **Customer profile** – age, class, disposable income, family size or geographic location. People living in large towns will have different requirements for wellington boots than those people living in rural locations. Customer profile is the most popular form of segmentation. An example may be where an organization may divide the country into North, South, East and West and them look at the profile of customers in each region based on their age or income. This is also known as demographic segmentation.
- **Lifestyle and personality** – where an individual aspires to a brand image or associates with a lifestyle trend. Customers want to be associated with the product or service and what is says about them. This is one of the reasons why some products are promoted very successfully on brand image such as Nike, Levi or Mercedes and can command a high price as part of the image.

Think

What brand or lifestyle do you associate yourself with?
Why is this?

- **Behavioural** – customers are segmented based on their knowledge, attitudes, uses or responses to a product. It will include the customers' perceived benefits sought by the product, when it is bought, why it is bought and the customers' beliefs and perceptions about the product. Segmentation on a behavioural basis is probably the most important segmentation variable. In simple terms a face-to-face seller could segment his customer base by defining which of his clients were enthusiastic about his product and therefore more likely to buy, those that were indifferent and those that were hostile and not likely to buy and split his time between them accordingly. He may wish to spend more time with the indifferent customers than the hostile customers knowing that he is more likely to get a sale in the longer term.

Question

How does your organization segment its customer base?

The databases that organizations hold containing customer data can be interrogated to discover many of the details of the customer profile so that different segments can be identified. Some of the lifestyle, personality and behavioural segmentation will be more difficult to assess depending on the nature of the information held about customers. This may not always be the case. as certain organizations will know that a customer buys from them for lifestyle reasons, with companies like Ikea or Habitat, or because there is a behavioural reason, for example Thornton's chocolate know they will make more sales at Christmas and Easter when it is traditional to give chocolate as a present.

It is also possible to segment the existing customer base by value of the account, ie how many products/services the customer has bought. Generally, an organization's customer base will follow the Pareto or 80/20 rule. This says that 20% of an organization's customers generate 80% of the profits. The aim therefore is to identify these extremely profitable customers and do everything possible to retain them and maximize their value. These customers may also be the ones that you are prepared to spend a little longer attending to their service requirements.

6.3 Buyer behaviour

We have looked at how organizations market their products and services to customers and how they try to ensure that customers receive the information that is relevant to them and their needs and wants. Let us now look at what factors will influence a customer when they make a purchase. These are as follows.

- **Personal** – an individual will relate a want or need to a product/service and will therefore make a purchase believing that it will satisfy that need or want. An example of this would be that a loan would help a customer purchase the new car they wanted. This is often referred to as a personal factor. Other personal factors could include how much money an individual will have left after paying all their bills, whether they are single or married, what their role is in the family and how many dependents they have.

- **Psychological** – this is based on a person's past experiences, beliefs and attitudes. In the example of a car purchase, a customer may think that a Ford is the best make of car because they have bought Ford before and found it to be reliable. It is difficult to change attitudes in people, so from a marketing perspective it is more desirable to design products or services that fit the attitudes.

- **Social** – social factors play a huge part in persuading a customer to choose a particular product or service over another. Quite often a buyer is influenced by a friend or family member's preference for a particular product/service. In the example of a car purchase the customer's friends may have told him that a specific make of car is more reliable so they may be tempted to try it out.

- **Cultural** – what a customer's beliefs are will influence what they buy. Customer's attitudes and beliefs are based around attitudes to religion, age, family and marriage and will affect the product/service that they buy. It is the pressure exerted by society at large and trends in fashion that will influence people in a more subconscious way. In the car example the customer may believe that now they have two children that an MPV type of car would be the right choice for them rather than a sports car, because they believe it is a more acceptable for family life.

Two people with the same needs can go through the buying process but may end up with two different products because of the different factors that shape their behaviour. The customer goes through a decision process when considering a purchase and it will vary in length depending on whether the customer is a 'deliberate' or 'compulsive' buyer. The customer may not make the decision alone and may be influenced by a number of people. This process is as in Figure 10.

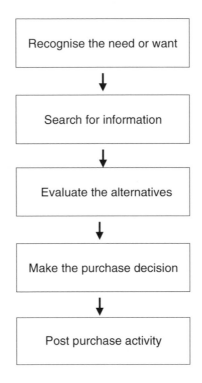

Figure 10: *The buying process*

Question

Where do you search for information when you start thinking about making a large and important purchase?

You are most likely to look for help from those people close to you such as family, friends or colleagues when thinking about making a large and important purchase. This information will be particularly useful if they have experience of the product or service you are considering buying. These are known as personal sources. You may then look for general information from the press or specialist magazines – public sources. You may look at advertising, brochures or websites of different companies who offer the product and even visit a showroom to talk to a salesperson. Whilst doing this you could even try out the product –an experimental source. This information search will be very personal to you and will depend on your prior experience, whether you have bought the product before, the size, importance and complexity of the purchase. Buying a tin of baked beans is not so important or complex as buying a house. In house buying the risks are higher than in doing the weekly shopping.

Question

What factors do you take into consideration when you are comparing different products to purchase?

When comparing different products you will probably consider some or all of the following:

- the product features such as its price, what it can do, its quality and styling;
- the relative importance of each of these features, for example when considering a new TV, picture quality might be more important than the sound quality;
- your perception of the image of each of the brands on offer, Sony might be considered a better brand of TV than a more obscure brand; and
- how you intend to use each of the features and what the benefits are to you. So for someone who is hard of hearing and uses the teletext facility when they watch TV, the sound quality may be of little interest to them at all.

The first two stages are where organizations are able to influence the decisions that customers make and this will be looked at in more detail in the next section. Once the customer has evaluated the information they will make their decision and purchase the product they believe is right for them. Once bought they will use and experience the product or service. They will make a judgement against their expectations, which will influence their post purchase behaviour and feelings. If they are happy they are likely to recommend the product to their friends, however, if they are not, they may complain and will tell friends of their bad experience.

6.4 Influencing buyer behaviour

Although an organization cannot directly control many of these influencing factors, it needs to understand the impact that they can have. The organization can then develop a marketing mix strategy that will appeal to the preferences of the target market. The following describes what organizations and individual employees can do to take advantage of each stage of the process.

6.4.1 *Need recognition*

The organization should be aware of the current needs of its customers as well as insufficiently developed or satisfied needs. In the case of service from financial services providers one of the prime reasons for customers changing providers is because they are dissatisfied with the levels or service they are receiving. Customer facing employees are in a prime position to pinpoint unsatisfied customer needs from comments that may come out in conversations with customers.

6.4.2 *Information search*

As we have seen in the last section different purchases require different levels of information. Organizations can take advantage of this by putting information on their websites and making literature readily available to customers. Direct mail is a way of targeting certain customers with product information if it is likely to be relevant to them, however, this can be quite a costly exercise for the organization if not done in a focused way. Customer-facing employees can help customers with information searching by ensuring that they answer questions correctly and offer other information about the product or service that the customer may not be aware of. It is also important for advisers to ask questions that will encourage the customer to discuss their requirements in more detail so that the best match can be found.

6.4.3 *Evaluation of alternatives and purchase decisions*

These parts of the process are where the customer goes away to think about what they want to do and will probably not welcome intrusion at this point. There would be no harm in the adviser making a follow-up contact to check whether the customer required any more help before making their final decision.

6.4.4 *Post purchase activity*

This is where good quality service is paramount. Depending on the way the customer has been treated during the buying process they will either recommend the organization to their friends and buy again, or take action that involves not buying again, telling their friends not to buy, making a complaint or worse taking legal action. The organization can contribute to making post-purchase customer service positive by having good systems and processes in place. An example of this is by having advisers that are polite, friendly, knowledgeable and able to undertake customer instructions accurately. Doing this will improve customer loyalty and increase the number of referrals of new customer to the organization.

As the process of acquiring customers is expensive, understanding buyer behaviour and why customers buy is very important. Considering all the marketing expenses such as advertising, direct mailing and customer segmentation it will not be surprising to find that many customers are unprofitable when first acquired. Often first-year acquisition activities can be thought of as an investment for the future. If the customer can be retained beyond the first year then sales from the second year and beyond often are profitable. This is the return on the investment made by the organization in that first year. Once the relationship is established it is therefore much easier to sell other products and services. Managing the customer relationship is the focus of the next unit.

6.5 Summary

Defining the customer market is a key exercise in marketing the products or services of an organization. It enables understanding of what is being offered to whom and how best to promote it. Segmentation ensures that the organization can focus its efforts in the right direction without spending time and resource on customers who are not and never will be buyers for their products/services. Being aware of buyer behaviour and what influences the prospective customer is a useful tool in influencing the buying decision. Both the marketing department and the customer facing employee need to be conscious of these when designing or undertaking the sales and service processes.

Unit 7

Managing customer relations

The aim of this unit is to enable you to:

- state the importance of managing customer relationships, and
- describe the need for quality service.

In this unit we will examine why customer management is important and in particular the issues relating to the customer attraction process. Once the customer has been acquired there are various customer management strategies that can be used to retain that customer and make the relationship profitable. Most organizations in the financial services sector use customer relationship management software to do this and we will see that it has a variety of functions that span across the whole organization.

The role of the contact centre adviser is key in managing these relationships on a one-to-one basis. Their general style of interaction and way in which they deal with customers is essential to the quality of the service delivered. A 'quality' culture is something that all organizations should strive for and we will consider the concept of quality and culture in some detail. Measuring quality can be problematic, particularly in a service environment, and we will have an overview of some of the proprietary external measures and then some of the internal quality measures that can be used. At the end of this unit we will consider some of the quality service issues within a contact centre environment, including customer satisfaction surveys, queuing time, complaint monitoring and what the adviser can do to enhance the customer experience.

7.1 Why customer management is important

We have seen in the last unit that customer attraction activities are expensive. The customer attraction process is as in Figure 11.

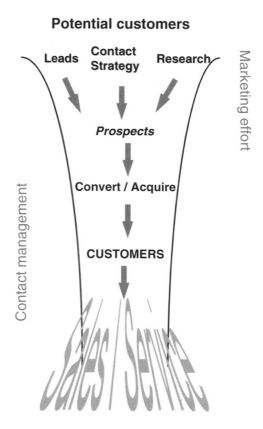

Figure 11: *Customer attraction process*

The process works in the same way as a funnel. In this example potential customers go into the top of the funnel and can be found from the existing customer base to be targeted for a new service. This can be done by a variety of means; from leads that advisers have identified during their telephone conversations with customers, from contact strategy, eg direct mailing, and from research from account information. As the customer drops down the funnel the organization needs to manage their progress. This may be by sending information about how their application is progressing or by adviser contacts to ask for further details. Customers are lost as they go through the funnel for a variety of reasons. It may well be that when they have all the information they need they decide the service isn't what they want or that they find a better offer elsewhere. Those that do sign up and use the service become customers and come out of the funnel as shown in Figure 11. The funnel technique enables the organization to pinpoint those customer that are genuinely interested and therefore the most likely to buy.

From a forecasting perspective the funnel is useful because it is possible to track how many people are going through, where and why they fall out, and how many appear at the bottom. For future campaigns it is then possible to estimate how many prospects are required at the top, the best ways of managing them and how many are likely to convert to the new service. It is also then possible to track how a campaign is progressing, whether it is on budget and if it is producing the expected revenue. You can see, however, that this requires much time, effort and resource.

So therefore once a customer has been gained it is important that they are retained. If managed well customers will:

- be more prepared to buy cross-sold products and services;
- have more confidence and trust in the organization;
- be more satisfied with the service received, so referring new customers to the organization; and
- feel as if they are important to the organization and are being treated as an individual.

For the organization this means there will be:

- increased profitability from the same customer base;
- improved communication with customers making relationships even stronger;
- cost containment; and
- improved brand value and image.

If the customer management process is not administered well then this will have a negative effect. Dissatisfied customers will drift away and this dissatisfaction goes unmonitored and unnoticed. This then means that improvements to service are not made and revenue is lost. The organization loses its external focus and then becomes vulnerable to the competition. The high 'churn' (acquisition and loss turnover) rate of customers creates additional cost on the organization. The organization and its employees have a situation where events appear out of their control.

For advisers the benefits of good customer management, of which they are an integral part, are many. A better relationship with customers means that they will be happier and this creates a less stressful environment. It then becomes easier to deal with problems; there is less fire-fighting and improved morale. Advisers achieve their performance and appraisal objectives and are rewarded better bonuses. Overall the performance of the contact centre improves and is able to contribute more to the organization's aims.

7.2 Customer management strategies

The latest thinking in customer management is the installation of customer relationship management (CRM) software. This software has a number of benefits as described in 7.1, however, it is important to not only have the system but also the business ethos to match it. The employees using the system have to believe that customer management is important or else they will just 'go through the motions' and not be committed to delivering excellent service and sales.

Whatever system is used there are probably three main reasons for its introduction:

- *increased sales revenue* – as in the customer attraction process in Figure 11, acquiring new customers, increasing market share, up-selling (ie selling more products to the same customers) is important;
- *customer retention* – this is about protecting existing revenue streams and improving the quality of service; and
- *cost reduction* – this entails streamlining processes, reducing the cost of serving low-value/high-cost customers. For example having an adviser knowledge base integrated with CRM can save up to 50 seconds on the average call length.

Whichever strategy the CRM system is installed to implement then it has to be supported by a segmentation policy as described in section 6.1 so that sufficient focus can be achieved.

One of the main benefits of a CRM system is that it can join together many disparate parts of the organization and improve internal communication. It makes the management of interactions across multiple communications channels of the web, contact centres, field sales and any partner networks that much simpler. This in turn improves the customer experience and their ability to 'one-stop-shop'. This will clearly improve accessibility and convenience for the customer. Figure 12 shows how the various parts of the organization can be joined using a CRM system.

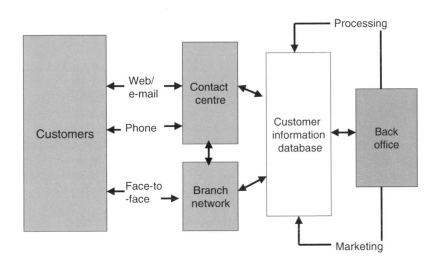

Figure 12: *Integrated systems*

In addition to integration there are some other problems that CRM can help overcome. If advisers have to use too many applications and screens this wastes time. It takes longer to train these different systems, so therefore it would be better to have just one system that is quick and easy to use and train to use. If advisers have to use paper forms to record information and then pass them on to someone else to key in, then this wastes time and can lead to errors. CRM systems can be set up to have on-screen workflows that are able to update databases in real-time. If advisers have to refer to paper records for product information or put customers on hold while they conduct research then this wastes time, can lead to incorrect information being given out and does not create a good impression. Online information systems, which are part of the CRM functionality, can overcome this type of issue.

As was seen in Unit 4, information is very useful and it is important to make the most of data collected from customers. In terms of customer data, CRM systems can help on each step of the data processing path.

1. Gather information about the customer.
2. Use data about the customer and appropriate products or services.
3. Create data about the interaction (eg customer history notes).
4. Analyse the data for example for potential future sales.
5. Apply what has been learnt about the data, perhaps in the next marketing campaign.

Various CRM applications allow this to be done in a number of ways, outlined below.

- **Contact management**: all contacts with the customer can be recorded and seen by everyone in the organization, so it creates a single view of the customer and collects data for advanced analysis, for example by the marketing function.
- **Workflow**: this is about routing the contact to the right adviser and what that adviser does with the customer. For example should there be a particular script that the adviser uses, or should the customer get a follow-up e-mail as a result of the contact.
- **Sales force automation**: this is the part of the system that tracks the customer acquisition process as in Figure 11. There are also additional functions that advisers could use as part of the acquisition process, such as scripts for follow-up contacts.
- **Service functions:** with sales comes service and such benefits are tracking complaints and their resolution.
- **Knowledge base**: as we have said knowledge bases improve the performance of advisers and this functionality will often bring together many of the internal resources that are available to advisers under one portal.
- **Telemarketing**: for an outbound contact centre this plays a key role. The functions of a CRM system will include lead management, campaign management, scripting and reporting.

For the organization a CRM application can mean that customer interactions can be managed more effectively and efficiently. It will mean that standards of service can be met within service level agreements, and be of the quality that is expected. It makes training of advisers more straightforward, giving them more confidence earlier. Internal communication is improved as employees find it uncomplicated to treat each other as customers. Customers have the right impression and customer satisfaction should improve. This improves customer retention over time and reduces cost in the longer term.

One of the early criticisms of CRM systems was that they failed to deliver their initial promises. Many organizations were hasty in implementing solutions that led to a mass of customer data that did not relate directly to any products or services. Whilst it has been difficult for organizations to quantify the return on investment, they are continuing to invest. This is partly because there is a new generation of CRM system called 'analytics'. This type of system analyses customer data combined with computerized logical reasoning to predict the most suitable products for customers. It also can make decisions on how individual customers' circumstances may affect their needs, wants and future behaviour. Imagine that a customer has a baby. This may mean that the household loses one income and may therefore have increased borrowing requirements in the short term or they may be more receptive to talk about insurance to provide for dependents. Analytics means that customers will no longer be pushed products and services at random, which will lead to reductions in cost and improved customer satisfaction.

7.3 Advisers and customer management

Advisers have a key role to play in managing the customer relationship. They have a duty to all customers to uphold the quality standards set by the organization (more about this in later sections of this unit) and the service levels that enable the centre to manage resources effectively. This ensures that all customers receive a similar level of service. Their general style of interaction and way in which advisers deal with customers is important.

Question

How would you describe a good adviser style when dealing with telephone contacts?

A good adviser style when dealing with customers over the telephone would be courteous, friendly, knowledgeable, able to listen and understand and have empathy with the customer's situation. Having empathy means that if a customer telephones to advise that their partner has died and needs their details removing from the account, that the adviser adjusts their behaviour to suit the grave situation. Conversely, if a customer telephones to say that they had just got married, then the adviser could change their behaviour to a congratulatory up-beat tone. An adviser who treats every customer in the same way whatever the situation, indicates that they are not really taking the customer's feelings or needs into account.

This ability to treat people as individuals is a crucial link in understanding both internal and external customers. Information collected by advisers enables the organization to have a greater understanding and personal insight into the needs of the customer. Advisers are the voice or word of the organization and for each customer contact are the organization's sole representative. For employees to offer a good service to the organization's customers they must feel that they have the knowledge, skills and tools to do this. To be able to create good customer relations an organization must ensure that the employees are motivated and stay motivated. The attitude of employees will come across to customers via their tone and pace of delivery irrespective of the individual's ability to do the job.

Another way in which advisers can build relationships with customers is by acknowledging information about the customer and building it into the conversation. Technology that enables advisers to see customer history information on screen as they talk enables the adviser to make reference to this in the conversation. If for example the customer has taken a loan for a new car then the adviser can ask how the new car is going which will make the customer feel as if the individual is genuinely interested in them and more likely to remain loyal as a result. In this way advisers can spot more opportunities for cross sales by improving their knowledge of individual customers and their lifestyles.

The ability of an adviser to solve customer problems as part of customer relationship management is key. Listening, understanding and asking the right questions before finding the right solution is essential. Even if the adviser doesn't know the answer they need to be prepared to apologise to the customer and say either that they will find out, or pass the customer to the most appropriate person to find out. An adviser with a positive attitude to problem solving will be better at dealing with customers that one who has a 'not my job' mentality.

Customer complaints are one of the biggest opportunities that advisers have of turning a negative experience of the organization into a positive one.

Question

What can an employee do to turn around a customer complaint?

There are a number of things that advisers can do to turn around a customer complaint. Again listening carefully is vital if the customer is to be understood and dealt with appropriately and satisfactorily. Not listening to a customer will lead to misunderstandings and frustration. This could ultimately lead to a complete breakdown in the communication. Putting the customer at ease and having the ability to understand what is being said shows an appreciation of the customer's point of view. Being patient with the customer also allows the individual to accurately pinpoint and resolve any issues. It is important to acknowledge where errors have been made and apologise for them. Customers should always be reassured that complaints will be dealt with and given a detailed explanation of how and when they will be resolved. Customers should be kept up-to-date, particularly when the complaint cannot be resolved immediately. Advisers have to watch their own energy levels when dealing with a high volume of complaints as they can soon become tired. The management should allow for more or longer break times if there are high volumes of complaints to be handled.

If advisers are in a sales role it is important that they match the right product to the right customer, rather than having a 'grapeshot' approach to selling. Unfortunately some of the reward systems used for sales advisers encourage them to ask insufficient questions and take short cuts to make a sale. This can lead to customers resenting the intrusion and this is detrimental to the customer relationship.

Advisers and any other customer-facing individuals are invaluable to any company and should never be underestimated in the management of customer relationships. Individuals are at the forefront of implementing and satisfying customer requirements. It is important that advisers have the right levels of training and incentives invested in them to ensure that they feel ready and able to do what is required of them.

7.4 Effects of good relationship management

There are a number of ways in which good customer relationships can be maintained. This can be done by ensuring that service levels are met, customers do not have to wait too long and when they do get through to an adviser they are dealt with appropriately. This means that there has to be the correct number of advisers to deal with volumes with the right skill sets and attitude. This is coupled with good products and services that make an attractive customer proposition. Underlying this will be effective use of automation and technology. The use of technology should be about improving the service and quality of the customer experience not purely about on cost cutting.

These efforts to improve customer relationships should lead to improved customer retention and therefore a better market share. By reducing acquisition costs and improving customer retention rates it reduces overall cost for the organization. This should therefore bring should bring enhanced competitive advantage, brand and image – success tends to breed success. It also makes the organization less vulnerable to either takeover or loss of customers to competitors.

Customers that are satisfied with their purchase or the service they have received are more likely to buy again and also more likely to recommend the organization to friends, family and work colleagues. Recommendations will undoubtedly improve a company's reputation and bring with it new customers and an increase in revenue and profit if costs are contained.

From an internal perspective good relationships between the organization and its employees will present itself to the customer. The employee will have an understanding of the kind of service they should be delivering because they feel valued and appreciated. It is easier to be professional with customers if behind the scenes all is well.

A company therefore that can prove to customers that it has a reputation for good customer satisfaction and customer loyalty is a company that can enhance its chances of a long and profitable existence.

Good relationships that the organization has worked hard to achieve can, and do, go wrong.

Question

What can make a customer relationship go wrong?

There are a number of factors that can undermine a customer relationship.

- Communication is key to running any type of organization and it is imperative that this does not stop or fail. Not communicating can seriously damage any relationship whether built up over a short or long period of time. Frequently, relationship problems start because the needs or wants of the customer are not listened to.
- Poor quality products, those that are not good value for money or those that fail to fully meet the needs of the customer can damage the customer relationship. The company may pursue what the customer feels is an inappropriate policy, for example where new customers are offered better interest rate deals that existing customers have no access to. This can really adversely affect levels of trust and customer loyalty as the customer then feels that their loyalty to the organization is not valued.
- Where a customer receives bad service or actions the customer has asked to be carried out are either not done or errors are made.
- Poorly trained advisers that have a poor attitude can also be highly detrimental to the smooth running of the centre. Contact centres that present calls to advisers who do not have the correct skills will leave customers feeling annoyed and frustrated.
- Where the technology or systems are not sufficient to handle to volume and nature of enquires, leading to dropped calls and requests that cannot be dealt with.
- Unresolved queries and complaints that are either left in queues or where advisers are unable to reach a satisfactory conclusion with a customer where a problem has arisen.
- External pressures such as poor media coverage can adversely affect the organization where customers take away their business as a result.

The effect of all these issues, ultimately, is that customers lose confidence in the product or service and they may feel rejected, unhappy and resentful. The result could lead to loss or cancellation of orders and the potential damage to future business. Over time the organization's image and reputation will be eroded leading to loss of income, profit, the exit of good employees to find better prospects and potentially the sale of that part of the business. The loss of customers, particularly if the organization does not find out why customers cancel orders, reduces the insight into how the product or service is performing and how it could be improved. If the organization itself is starting to fail it may even reach the point where it has neither the resources nor the expertise to put these things right. Companies that chose not to spend the time communicating with customers and employees will find that management of these relationships becoming increasingly difficult with dire consequences.

7.4.1 Summary

In these last four sections we have seen how important it is to manage relationships and how strategies such as CRM can help streamline processes, provide more complete customer information and lead to more profitable customer relationships, whilst decreasing operating costs. A computer-driven system can improve marketing campaign rates and reduce customer acquisition costs. It enables more quick and efficient delivery to the customer, so shortening the sales cycle and improving customer satisfaction. Advisers have the tools to be able to handle contacts more quickly and thereby have the capability to improve customer retention. We have seen that customer management is key to the success of both the adviser and the organization.

7.5 'Quality' culture

In these last three sections of this unit we are going to explore quality in the contact centre environment. We will look at what quality culture is and why we might want it. We will then explore some of the different ways of measuring quality and some of the issues with providing service in a contact centre environment. Key to this, as with managing customer relations, and very closely linked to this topic area, is the role of the contact centre adviser.

Having a 'quality' culture is something that many organizations would like to say about themselves. The need for quality is regularly cited as important for an organization to strive for. By having better 'quality' than other organizations will clearly give a competitive advantage. It will also be one of the most visible parts of what the organization does. It is clearly a major influence on customer satisfaction or dissatisfaction. Advertising will promote this desire, however what does it really mean and does the organization actually achieve it?

Question

What does quality mean?

Very simply quality means 'doing things right'. This means not making mistakes. It means satisfying customers by providing error-free products and services, which are fit for their purpose and meet the customer needs. What these things are depends very much on the operation that the organization runs and the business it is in.

Supermarket
- Goods are fresh and displayed attractively
- The store is clean, tidy and well-decorated
- The trolleys are easy to push around the shop
- The staff are friendly and helpful

New house
- Structurally sound and complies with building regulations
- Nicely decorated and finished off properly
- Kitchen and bathroom appliances work properly
- Well laid out garden

Contact Centre
- Technology systems reliable
- It is possible to connect to an adviser quickly if you need to
- Advisers knowledgeable, friendly and courteous
- Advisers deal with queries first time, so there is no need to call back

---

Figure 13: *Quality could mean...*

Figure 13 shows what quality could mean for three different scenarios. You can see that it is different for the supermarket manager, the house builder and the contact centre manager. You will also see that there are differences with what quality means depending on whether there are products or services, or a mixture of the two involved.

By having quality inside the operation, whatever that might be, not only leads to external customer satisfaction but it also makes life easier inside the organization too. So satisfying internal customers by providing a high quality internal service as is important as satisfying external ones.

Quality reduces mistakes. The fewer mistakes made, the less time needs to be spent correcting them. There will be less confusion and irritation. For example, if the supermarket's regional warehouse sends the incorrect goods then someone will have to sort out the error, arrange for the goods to be shipped back and the right goods delivered. This wastes time and cost. This is not the only impact of this error. It could mean that there are insufficient goods on the shelves and customers go away empty-handed. This means a loss of revenue and perhaps the customer deciding to shop at a competitor store the next week. If management are constantly spending time on sorting out mistakes this means that they have little time to be proactive in their own role, which means that they are not focusing on managing the business.

Question

What do we mean by culture?

Culture is the 'way things are done around here'. It can have informal aspects such as the stories people tell about the organization and whether these stories are positive or negative. A positive story could be how a quality job received managerial praise, a negative story could be about how someone got away with a poor job and cheated the system. Another informal aspects would be the power structures, ie how power is distributed within the organization and what are the blockers, and symbols, so what language and internal jargon is used, what the status symbols are perceived to be.

Formal aspects would be about routines and rituals. For example what to training programmes emphasize (this should be quality) and what routines would look odd if they were changed. Control systems are formal structures, so what is monitored and controlled, if is there a focus on reward or punishment. If the reward system gives credit for quantity of contacts handled rather than quality, this is what advisers will focus on. The organization's structure, whether it is flat or hierarchical and whether it encourages internal competition or collaboration can be another sign.

There is not really a good or bad culture as such. The issue is more about whether the culture itself supports quality. There may be a desired culture driven by senior management, however there may be a gap between what is desired and what actually is in place. As with changing any attitudes an organization's culture will take time to change and if an organization decides it wants to embark on installing a culture that revolves around quality it will take time to achieve, particularly if there are high levels of mistakes and re-work already. They may wish to use a quality system and we will look at this in the next section.

Question

What might motivate an organization to want a quality system?

The senior management of an organization may want to install a quality system for a variety of reasons. They would first have to define why they were looking for such as system. They would have to be clear on the problems or issues that were to be addressed. The advantages of using such a system would need to be explored and what would it offer that couldn't be better achieved by improving existing performance management systems. They would also have to consider all the stakeholders and what their views were. It may be that benchmarking against other organizations is important and so that they could strive to achieve 'best in class' status. It may be to receive a kite mark so that customer confidence could be improved. Some organizations have to have certain quality standards to enable them to tender for large contracts. At the very least it would be to improve customer satisfaction and brand image.

7.6 Measuring quality

There are many different ways in which quality can be measured. Depending what the nature of the business is and what is considered important will impact on this measurement. There will need to be some questions that should be considered before any quality scheme is embarked on by contact centre management. These questions may be as follows.

- What are we trying to achieve?
- What would be considered to be a successful outcome?
- What will be the benefits for the organization and our employees?
- How important is external recognition? Do we want to have internal self-assessment or external accreditation?
- Does anyone else in other parts of the organization have experience we can draw on?

- Who will manage the quality process?
- How much will it cost?
- How much time will it take?
- How will we measure the benefits?

We will now look in outline at a number of schemes that could be applicable in a contact centre environment.

7.6.1 The Excellence Model – British Quality Foundation

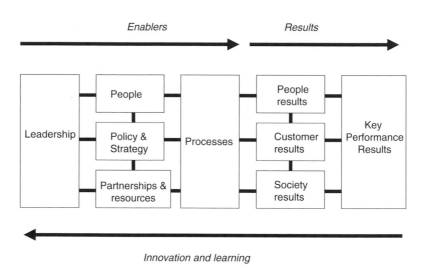

Figure 14: *The Excellence Model framework*

Figure 14 shows the nine different components of the Excellence Model. These components have been identified as the key components of business excellence and have been verified by extensive research and validation by several hundred organizations throughout Europe. The 'enablers' are concerned with what is done to run the organization and how it is operated. The 'results' are concerned with what the organization has achieved and is achieving as seen by the various stakeholders. The diagram shows the basic premise of the model that; customer results, people results and corporate social responsibility are achieved through leadership driving policy and strategy, people, partnership and resources ultimately leading to excellence in key performance results.

Performance against the model is used to judge entries for the UK Business Excellence Award, however organizations can take the first step of self-assessing against the model to identify strengths and areas for improvement.

7.6.2 BSI British Standards

The aim of the standards is to make life safer and efficient and to smooth the progress of trade. The standards cover a very wide range of areas from technical guidelines from the aerospace industry to specifications for making things happen, eg in the management of customer loyalty. British Standards Institute (BSI) is the national standards body for the UK and is responsible for facilitating, drafting, publishing and marketing the British Standards and other guidelines. The most popular management system series is ISO 9000. BSI provides organizations with independent third-party accreditation of their management systems. ISO 9001:2000 relates to quality specifically.

When an organization has the ISO accreditation it gives purchasers the confidence that capability of achieving good quality. It does not however guarantee that they will receive a good quality output from suppliers.

7.6.3 Investors in People (IiP)

This is the national standard that sets out a good level of practice for training and development of people to achieve business goals. The standard was developed during 1990 by the National Training Task Force in partnership with leading national businesses, personnel, professional and employee organizations such as the Confederation of British Industry (CBI), Trades Union Congress (TUC) and the Chartered Institute of Personnel and Development (CIPD).

The standard provides a national framework for improving business performance and competitiveness through a planned approach to setting and communicating business objectives and developing people to meet these objectives. The result is what people can do and are motivated to do matches with the organization needs them to do. The standard also ensures the quality of internal processes and procedures for people management.

The IiP standard is based on four key principles:

- commitment to invest in people to achieve business goals;

- planning how skills, individuals and teams are to be developed to achieve these goals;
- taking action to develop and use necessary skills in a well-defined and continuing programme directly tied to business objectives; and
- evaluation outcomes of training and development for individuals' progress towards the goals, the value achieved and future needs.

Every three years IiP reviews the standard to ensure that it is still relevant, accessible and beneficial to organizations of all types and sizes and also to ensure that the experience of using the standard provides real added value to those organizations.

7.6.4 Plain English Campaign – Crystal Mark

The Plain English Campaign is an independent group that promotes the writing of public information in plain English. This means that the intended audience can understand and act upon this information from a single reading. In 1990 the Crystal Mark was introduced to encourage organizations to communicate clearly with the public and therefore improve the quality of that communication.

The Crystal Mark has now become firmly established in the UK as the standard that all organizations aim for when producing public information. Their standards cover such areas such as average sentence lengths, everyday English, conciseness, typeface, layout and line length. It covers documents such as books, brochures, websites and computer software. Every item that has passed the assessment can carry the Crystal Mark logo to confirm its quality.

7.6.5 Internal systems

There are a number of internal systems that an organization could create to make its own bespoke quality programme. A number of suggestions are outlined below.

- *Customer charter* – the contact centre will run to a service level through the Erlang calculations for resourcing. This could be built into a 'customer charter', eg 'we promise to answer all calls within three rings' which is made known to customers and so they know what level of quality is being aimed for.

- *Customer satisfaction surveys* – internal quality can be measured by undertaking customer satisfaction surveys, more about this in the next section.
- *Accreditation of training* – internal training programmes can be accredited to external professional bodies, eg the Institute of Financial Services, to show that they meet industry standards and employees can be recognized for completion by more than just their employer.
- *Competency frameworks to assess skills and behaviour* – this would be a specifically designed range of skills and behaviours that can be used for appraisal and people development. The competency framework shows what is required by all employees to perform well in their role so giving a focus for good performance. Typically this type of model is not based on call handling statistics and so therefore gives team managers an objective standard to work to when undertaking observe and coach sessions.
- *Knowledge testing* – when learning about new products and services advisers can undergo knowledge testing to show they have acquired the right amount of information to talk to customers without making errors.
- *Supporting employees in the completion of awards* – if part of the people policy is to develop individuals through external awards then this can be supported through monetary support and time off for study. This improves the quality of the people by widening their horizons and motivating them to progress through the organization, so having a positive impact on morale.

7.7 Issues with providing quality service

In this section we will look at some of the specific issues related to providing a quality service in the contact centre environment. From Unit 5, section 4 you will remember that the features of service were:

- intangibility;
- inseparability;
- perishibility; and
- heterogeneity (or variability).

These features mean that service is can be difficult to measure and providing that service also, at times, problematic. In a contact centre environment the adviser/customer interaction is key, so differences in advisers' and customers' personality and behaviours will mean that each interaction however similar in initial purpose could have a variety of different outcomes however well the adviser handles it. However much the advisers are trained to be consistent and to follow processes customers have different backgrounds, views and experiences that change over time. This can make the measurement of customer satisfaction to measure quality rather subjective or biased, depending on how the research is carried out and which particular segment of customers is contacted.

Question

What are the issues with trying to measure customer satisfaction?

The measurement of customer satisfaction may be undertaken by a central marketing team through surveys or by team managers undertaking callbacks to customers that have recently talked to advisers. This could be seen as biased, so the organization could also employ an external agency to make telephone calls to customers to gain an independent view of the organization.

The next question is how many customers would make a reasonable sample, ie how many customers would you need to talk to before some general themes started to emerge. This could be as little as 5% of the customer base however many customers may need to be contacted to ensure that 5% could be engaged in conversation. This obviously could be quite a large task and not perhaps one therefore that the centre itself would have the resources to undertake.

The choice of media used for surveys has limitations. Consumers do not always respond well to telephone canvassing so a good script would be required to enable tele-researchers to gain the customers attention quickly. The response is immediate and it is quick and easy for the customer to respond in this way. Postal questionnaires tend to get put to one side, as they are seen as too time consuming to complete. They usually require some sort of incentivization to motivate customers to return them, which leads to additional cost. E-mail questionnaires are becoming more popular and would be useful for a provider that is web-based, however, they might not be suitable for a telephony provider, as not all its customers may have access to the Internet.

Once these issues had been overcome the design of the questionnaire has to be considered. They questions themselves can elicit either yes/no type answers or answers that require a qualitative response. This type of question may require the customer to choose one from a range of responses, eg:

'how do you rate the helpfulness of our advisers? Choose one from excellent, good, satisfactory, poor.'

Both of these types of questions will give a numeric result in that the response to each question can be given a value, eg 0 for no and 1 for yes, and the information the presented graphically.

If the questionnaire asked 'what did you like about our mortgage product?' it could produce a wide range of customer responses of a varying length. This type of information would have to be represented in large amounts of text, or highlighted comments. Both of these methods are time-consuming to prepare and to read in the final report. The way in which the data will be presented when all the responses have been received should be considered at the outset rather than at the end when a report is being compiled.

The areas of interest to the customer and the organization should be considered carefully as a questionnaire that takes too long to complete will not be completed. Therefore the topic areas and questions cannot be too many or too wide.

Usually if customers respond to a questionnaire that asks for their views on how service could be improved then they will expect something to happen as a result. The organization must therefore consider before it embarks on a customer satisfaction survey what action it would be prepared to take as a result of the survey. If no action is taken, not even the communication of the results in some way, then those customers that did take part will not feel as if their time was well spent.

Two of the main indicators for quality in a contact centre environment is queuing time and complaint handling. The ultimate goal of a queuing system is to manage and enhance the customer's involvement with the organization. Several recent surveys show that there is no one right answer for what should be used in a queuing system; no single piece of music, or number of rings, or information source that would suit all types of customer. Proactive use of a combination of the techniques according to information known about the customer can start to create the aura of involvement.

The queue content can be assessed according to customer profile by differentiating the callers into different segments, eg first-time callers, ordinary and premium customers and also differentiating between the call content, eg service or sales. For example first-time callers could be told about the website and its various features whilst existing customers could be informed of new services offered on the website. The caller could be given information, which is beneficial or interesting to their circumstances and, at the same time, promote the brand in a manner consistent with the corporate image.

Call queues need not be seen as an unfortunate but necessary evil of call flow dynamics where brand image and customer service is ignored. The quality of the queuing system can become an integral part of the customer contact strategy.

Complaint handling and the analysis of the nature and frequency of complaints can be a useful indicator of the quality of service (or lack of it).

Question

How would you analyse information relating to complaints to check on quality of the service in your contact centre?

The analysis of complaints could be around the following.

- How many customer complaints were received within the last month/ quarter?
- What is the trend, are the numbers going up or down?
- What percentage were repeat complaints?
- What were the complaints about, so percentages in areas such as:
  o waiting times;
  o problems with the Internet or systems access;
  o system down time;
  o the way in which the call was handled;
  o specific employees;
  o processing transaction times;
  o charges;
  o product/service features;
  o customer service levels not met?

This sort of feedback needs to collected and analysed regularly and action taken to correct errors that are made on an ongoing basis. If customer service levels have been promised these standards need to be monitored and tracked, and any deviation investigated.

The role of the adviser in delivering a quality service is therefore key. There are five factors that are essential to delivering a good quality service.

1. **Tangibles** – those things that are physical should send the right messages to customers. For a contact centre this could be the organization's website, brochures mailed in the post, the content and layout of e-mails and the accessibility to advisers.

2. **Reliability** – the adviser's ability to perform the services efficiently and effectively. The adviser needs to be able to communicate in a businesslike yet friendly and helpful manner. The chances are that the customer will recognize that the adviser has really listened, understood and appreciated their situation. The customer should be satisfied with the response and that all their concerns have been dealt with to their satisfaction.

3. **Responsiveness** – the adviser's willingness to help customers and provide a prompt service. Of course it is not always possible to fulfil every customer's requirements, so when this is the case the adviser needs to be creative in how they deal with this situation so as not to disappoint the customer.

Question

What can an adviser say to a customer when they cannot fulfil their requirements?

If an adviser isn't able to deal with a query they have a number of options.

- 'Unfortunately it's not possible for us to do that, however we can look at some alternatives for you'.
- 'That's not something that this company offers, however we do have some alternatives that you may wish to look at...'
- 'Sorry, I can't help with that but I can give you the details of someone who can help you'.
- 'I don't know the answer to that question, however if you would like to hold, I'll find out for you'.

By going that little bit further, gives customers' confidence and that the adviser has listened and tried to help.

4   **Assurance** – the adviser's knowledge and skill and their ability to inspire trust and confidence. The adviser needs to communicate in such a way so that the customer recognizes this. For example in a telephone contact the adviser that has a strong, positive tone will inspire more confidence than one who is quietly spoken and hesitant.

5   **Empathy** – the adviser's ability to show the customer that they can see the customer's perspective and be able to treat the customer as an individual. It enables the adviser to understand the customer's issue and not instantly judge the customers by their own views and standards. This one of the most essential communication skills.

Whatever framework is used for internal quality the team managers have a vital role in monitoring and developing adviser quality. With an appraisal system, perhaps using a competency framework, where the advisers know what skills and behaviours are required, their objectives and management towards those objectives can be transparent and fair. The management team should foster an open culture enabling individuals to learn from their mistakes. This enables advisers to take responsibility for their actions when things go wrong without the fear of retribution. This then leads to improved morale and motivation and contributes towards the 'internal quality' of the organization itself.

7.8 Summary

In these last three sections on quality we can see that having a focus on quality can put the right processes in place. It is vital that all employees believe in quality and are goaled in a way that supports this aim. If, for example, people are focused in a way that is relating purely to statistics such as call length and wrap time reduction, then it is likely that the quality of their customer interactions will suffer. The customer will know that they are being rushed and will not consider this to be a very good experience as it gives the impression that the adviser does not have time to listen to them.

The measurement of quality, whether this is organization-wide or for the contact centre specifically is something that requires careful consideration before implementation. Whether it is external accreditation or the creation of an internal system, there are a number of questions that need to be answered, particularly if there are budget considerations. Whatever route is taken it will take hard work to get it right and for the benefits to be seen. It often takes time to change perceptions especially of customers who have limited contact with the organization. As with measuring quality there are issues with providing it consistently and no organization can rest on its laurels saying 'we've done it!'. It requires continued effort and focus to maintain the standards achieved.

Unit 8

Customer relationships and the law

The aims of this unit are to enable you to:

- **describe the elements of law on which customers' rights are founded;**
- **describe the customer relationship.**

The final two units of this text are centred on giving you an understanding of the basic rights of customers when they deal with the contact centre. In this unit, we will examine the differences between the different types of law and how laws are created. Included are contract law and agency law in further detail and we will look at what remedies are available under them.

As the law relating to contact centres has not really been tested by the courts we will look at some of the industry guidelines that have been created to protect customers, particularly when they have a complaint. The legal implications of the customer relationship will be covered in terms of the banking relationship and the duties and rights of the organization in this. There are a number of codes laid out that financial service providers subscribe to that provide a framework for dealing with customers. The most notable of these is the Banking Code and the Mortgage Code, at which we will look in outline.

8.1 Elements of law

There are many different definitions of what the words 'the law' means. Some of these definitions are easier to understand than others.

Question

What do you think the words 'the law' mean?

Essentially the law is a set of rules instituted by Acts of Parliament, custom or practice applying to individuals or corporate bodies in order to deal with those who break the conventions of society. English law can be divided into criminal and civil law. The basic differences between them are explained below.

8.1.1 Criminal law

- Breaking the rules may result in prosecution of the offender.
- These rules deal with behaviour that the state disapproves of.
- Cases are heard in criminal courts – Magistrates' Court or the Crown Court.
- Punishment may include fines or imprisonment.
- The parties involved will be either the Crown or the police versus the defendant.

8.1.2 Civil law

- Breaking the rules may result in the offender being sued.
- These rules relate to disputes between individuals or corporate bodies.
- Cases are heard in civil courts – the County Court or the High Court.
- The parties involved are the plaintiff and the defendant.
- The defendant may have to pay compensation/damages to the plaintiff.

The English legal system has evolved gradually over a period of over 900 years and over this time has become increasingly more complex and detailed. This is why some of the terminology may seem old-fashioned in a modern context.

Law may be sub-divided into four main types, outlined below.

- **Common law** – this is a judge-made system of law originally based on local custom and now applied uniformly throughout England.

- **Equity** – equity literally means fairness or justice, therefore the essential point of equity is to establish what is fair in a particular case at the expense of technical niceties. This can sometimes be in conflict with common law however equity law will prevail.
- **Statute** – this is where an Act of Parliament creates a new rule of conduct. It is passed by Parliament and can only be repealed (cancelled) by Parliament. It is also known as 'legislation', it prevails over both common and equity law.
- **European Community (EC) law** – this is created by either regulations which are binding on all EC member states without Parliamentary legislation or by Directives which require member states to pass national laws within a certain time period. The European Court's view is that for as long as the UK is a member of the EC, then EC law overrides English Law where they are in conflict.

8.2 Contract law

The next section deals with the law of contract.

Question

How would you define a contract?

A contract can be described as an agreement between two or more parties, especially one that is written and enforceable by law to deliver goods or services or to do something on mutually agreed terms. Generally a contract may be written, oral or even 'implied' by conduct or action. This may be surprising as most people think a contract is a large and difficult document to read and understand. Some types of contract **must** be in writing and in a particular format, eg for the sale of land.

For a contract to be valid it must contain the following elements.

- **Offer and acceptance** – this means that there must be evidence that the first party made an offer of goods or services to the second party and that the second party accepted the conditions. It must be capable of being accepted without qualification (ie without special conditions attached, such as in house purchase, 'subject to survey') and be in specific terms. So the invitation to enter into a negotiation or to supply information does not form an offer and acceptance.

- **An intention to create a legal relationship** – this is a complex area, however, put simply, domestic agreements cannot be enforced unless there is proof of an intention to create legal relations. In commercial agreements it is presumed that the parties intend to make an agreement unless there is evidence that legal relations were not intended.

- **Consideration** – this is defined as any form of remuneration or encouragement of value given by one person to the other to persuade them to enter into the contract. More often than not this is in the form of money.

- **Capacity to contract** – a person's ability to enter into a legal contract may be affected by their contractual capacity. The main groups where valid contracts would become problematic are:
  o minors (those people under the age of 18);
  o persons who are insane or drunk;
  o registered companies – these are legal entities in their own right that are governed by their 'memorandum of association' which sets out, amongst other things, what powers to contract the company has. If the company enters into a contract which it does not have the power to do then the contract would be rendered void.

- **Reality of consent** – to be valid a contract must also have real consent by all parties to the contract. The contract may be rendered invalid by any misrepresentation, mistakes, duress (pressure or coercion), undue influence or fraud. Another point is that as a general rule persons who are not party to the contract cannot sue any of the parties to the contract concerning matters contained within it.

- **Legality of object** – it is not possible to make contracts which are illegal, for an immoral purpose, or which are contrary to public policy (broadly against public interest). For example there cannot be a contract to commit a criminal act.

Contracts may be valid, void, voidable or unenforceable. A **void** contract is one that is cancelled from the start as if it never existed. A **voidable** contract is one that continues to be valid until such time it is repudiated (rejected) by one of the parties, usually at the option of the injured party. An **unenforceable** contract is one that is valid except that it cannot be enforced by law by one of the parties should the other fail to fulfil their obligations.

The final area to consider in relation to contract law is how the contract may be terminated. A contract ends or is 'discharged' when the 'obligations' (duties or requirements) contained within it cease to be binding. This may occur in one of four ways:

- **by agreement** – if there is a subsequently a new contract or if there are clauses within it which trigger automatic discharge relating to a certain point in time or the occurrence of a particular event;
- **by performance** – if all the parties have met all their promises or obligations in full, on time and correctly then the contract will be discharged by performance such as the provision of a holiday by a travel company;
- **by frustration** – if it impossible for the obligations to be met that are due to circumstances beyond the control of the parties then the contracted is 'frustrated' (thwarted) and discharged. In our holiday example this could be by serious illness of the traveller, which is why many people take travel insurance;
- **by breach** – where promises have been made in the contract and they have been broken the innocent party to the contract can treat the contract as discharged.

Here is a simple example of a contract. Mr Smith agrees with Mr Jones to buy his lawnmower for £50 and they shake hands on it. Mr Jones believes therefore that Mr Smith will pay £50 on delivery of the lawnmower.

Question

Has there been offer and acceptance here?

There has been offer and acceptance.

Question

What is the consideration to be?

The consideration is £50.

Question

When will the contract be discharged?

The contract will be discharged when Mr Jones delivers the lawnmower and Mr Smith hands over £50.

In the commercial world where an individual consumer contracts with a large and powerful organization, the concept is that a contract is reliant on agreement. What can happen is that one party is in a better or stronger position than the other. The effect is that the organization can impose terms on the consumer. For example the majority of organizations will have a standard contract with terms and conditions of sale of its products and services. Customers will be bound under the terms and conditions of this contract, whether they are aware of them or not. It can be the case that customers are completely unaware that they have entered into an agreement or have done so unwillingly. This is why it is very important that customers' attention is brought to terms and conditions so that they can understand the nature of the agreement they are entering into. A person becomes a banking customer of a financial services provider as soon as an account is opened. Often the account opening form is the written contract that sets out the banker-customer relationship.

8.3 Agency law

An **agency** is in effect a contract whereby one person, the 'principal', contracts with another person, the 'agent', with the objective that the agent will act on behalf of the principal to undertake certain duties.

Question

What are common examples of agency?

Common examples of agency are those such as where an estate agent is hired to sell people's houses, where an auctioneer sells goods on behalf of the vendor, or where a financial services provider will act as for an insurance company selling their insurance products.

In the example of the estate agent there are three parties and two contracts. Consider person (A) is selling their house to purchaser (B) using estate agent (C). The two contractual relationships exist between:

- A as the vendor (seller) to B, the purchaser; and
- A as principal to C, the agent.

To be a valid agency relationship the principal must have full contractual capacity. The agent however does not need to have full contractual capacity.

An agency may be created verbally or by written agreement and may relate to one or a series of transactions. Essentially there are six ways of creating an agency, which are as follows.

- **By consent** – this may be by express or implied authority. An express authority is where the principal instructs the agent either verbally or in writing. In the estate agent example the agent would be instructed expressly in writing. An implied authority is where it is assumed that the agent has authority. Where such implied authority is usual then in law the principal will be liable for the agent's actions.
- **By statute** – this is where laws affect the formation of agency such as the Partnership Act 1980, where the partners are agents for each other.
- **By apparent authority** – this is where an agent exceeds his 'actual' authority. These actions however are of a type that an agent would normally have the authority to undertake. The principal is bound by the limits of either the actual or apparent authority whichever is the wider.
- **Of necessity** – this could be where there is an emergency and a decision has to be made. This type of agency can be established provided the following four conditions are met:
  o the agent has control of the property in question;
  o there was a real emergency;
  o the principal could not be contacted;
  o the agent acted honestly in the best interests of the principal.

  Imagine an example where Mrs Brown owns a coffee shop. She goes on holiday and employs a manager to run the shop whilst she is away. Unfortunately a water pipe bursts in the shop and, as Mrs Brown is trekking in the Himalayas, she cannot be contacted. The manager, out of necessity to the ongoing business of the coffee shop, can authorize a plumber to carry out the repairs and incur costs on Mrs Brown's behalf.
- **By ratification** – if a person has acted without authority but these actions are subsequently ratified or confirmed by the principal then the principal becomes bound by any transactions that have occurred.

The main duties of a principal are to:

- pay the agent for undertaking duties; and
- pay all related expenses and to indemnify (cover) the against loss, costs and liabilities in undertaking his/her duties.

In the contractual relationship between the principal and the agent the duties of one are the rights of the other. An agent has five main responsibilities to their principal, namely to:

- obey any instructions given by the principal;
- perform their duties personally, ie he cannot delegate his authority except in certain circumstances;
- use reasonable care and skill;
- act in good faith;
- keep proper accounts for inspection by the principal.

The ways of terminating an agency are similar to those discussed in contract law discussed in the last section.

Banks act as agents for their customers when they pay (debit from a customer's account) or collect (process a cheque paid into a customers account). The bank owes the customer a duty of care and may be liable if it pays away funds on a customer's cheque that have been fraudulently altered. We will examine the issue of professional negligence such as this in section 8.6.

8.4 Remedies available to customers

The last two sections explained the basis on which customer relationships are based. They are based on the various acts relating to contract law or the acts relating to agency law. There are a variety of remedies available to customers in terms of their relationship with the contact centre. We will first look at some of those from a legal perspective and some of the guidelines that financial services organizations will adhere to for the protection of their customers.

The Unfair Contract Terms Act 1977 and the Unfair Contract Terms Directive deal with the terms of certain contracts for the sale of goods. They are examples of where legislation can severely restrict the ability of providers and substantially protect the individual. The Act curtails the use of terms which try to exclude liability on the part of the provider and which try to restrict the rights of the individual. Contracts of insurance are exempt from this Act however they are subject to the Directive, which applies to life and pensions contracts. Any unfair term – one that causes significant imbalance in the parties' rights and obligations to the detriment of the customer – is not binding on the consumer, but the rest of the contract can continue to bind both parties.

The Supply of Goods and Services Act 1982 applies to all contracts involving the supply of services. It implies three terms into such contracts, which are:

- that the service will be performed with reasonable care and skill;
- if no time limit is set in the contract, work will be done in a reasonable time; and
- if no price is fixed a reasonable charge will be made.

If things do go wrong there are two types of remedies available for breach of contract, 'judicial' and 'non-judicial' remedies. Judicial remedies are those where the parties are required to go before a court of law or an arbitrator. Judicial remedies can also be divided again into criminal and civil remedies. Sometimes the same conduct may amount to a breach of contract as well as a criminal offence.

A breach of contract does not normally involve any criminal liability, simply a civil wrong, and will be concerned with civil remedies for breach. Under civil remedies the injured party can claim for specific relief, damages or restitution. For example, a customer (the injured party) may claim compensation because he believes that he has not received the agreed service from a company he has. Such compensation would take the form of a monetary payment.

A claim for 'restitution' can be applied when, for example, a customer has made a payment in advance but does not receive any goods from the supplier and may claim the return of his money. Whenever a contract is broken damages are always available and can be claimed as a right. Claims for damages differ from specific relief or restitution as these are left to the discretion of the court and other restrictions may be applied. The injured party does not have to prove any loss to be entitled to nominal damage claims.

Before a customer would consider taking the above type of action, particularly through the courts, then in the financial services industry it is usual for a customer to follow the organization's internal complaints procedure. Customers first would need to complain directly to their financial services provider and obtain the name of the person who will be dealing with their complaint. The customer should always make a note of the person they speak to and record the details of the conversation that took place. A copy of the internal complaints procedure must be provided to the customer within five business days of receipt of the complaint and to any customer on request.

It is recommended that customers should put their complaint in writing, as this sets out the exact nature of their problem and gives the provider an opportunity of responding and putting things right. Customers should always keep copies of any correspondence, should they need to refer to them at a later point.

If the customer is still not satisfied and their provider cannot offer a solution within eight weeks, the organization must issue a final response or notification. A position of 'deadlock' is said to be reached. At this point the customer may refer the complaint to the Financial Ombudsman Service (FOS). The FOS deals with complaints about most financial services products and services provided in the UK. This includes most financial organizations including banks, building societies, credit unions, insurance companies, pension providers, investment companies, stockbrokers and any other FSA authorized firms. The customer has six months from receiving the final response to taking their complaint to the FOS.

The FOS will look at the details of the case and ask for extra evidence if necessary. The FOS will then decide whether the complaint is justified and if so order the organization to put matters right. The FOS is able to make decisions that bind an organization to compensate the customer. Any compensation given will relate to the actual loss they have incurred. At present there is a maximum compensation limit of £100,000. Figure 15 overleaf gives an overview of this process.

You will see in Figure 15 that if the customer is still not happy with the FOS outcome they can take the matter to court. Customers are, however, advised that if an Ombudsman has not found in their favour then it is unlikely that a judge would overturn that judgment. The advantage to the customer of the FOS service is that this is free whereas going to court could be costly. In the main FOS decisions are made from the documentary evidence and customers are not expected to attend meetings, so saving the customer's time and any additional cost.

For regulation of the contact centre industry those providers that offer premium rate calls are regulated by ICSTIS, the Independent Committee for the Supervision of Standards of Telephone Information Services. This is an industry-funded non-profit making body that regulates the content and promotion of services through their Code of Practice. They are able to investigate complaints and have the power to fine organizations and bar

Customer makes an initial complaint and give the organization the chance to put things right

The organization gives the customer the name of the person who will handle the complaint. There should be a proper complaints procedure and the customer told how to use it.

If the complaints process reaches 'deadlock' the customer can take their grievance to the relevant independent complaints scheme usually the Financial Ombudsman Service (FOS)

The matters is either resolved by the FOS or, if the customer is still not happy, then the matter can be taken to court.

Figure 15: *Overview of complaints process*

access to services. The Code of Practice is regularly updated to take into account the pace of technological change.

8.4.1 Summary

The first four sections of this unit have dealt with the background legal and regulatory frameworks in which financial services contact centres deal with their customers. We will now go on to look at more specific duties and rights of customers, organizations and their employees.

8.5 Duties and rights of a customer

As we said at the beginning of this unit there has been little case law that has been fully tested which explores the duties and rights of customers in a contact centre environment. While contact centres provide a good service to customers, it is often on the basis that the customer has been given number and security codes by which he/she can be identified and the computer systems can process the customer's requests. It is important to understand that any breaches of confidentiality or misuse of the system is the customer's responsibility as much as the provider's.

The main Acts that are thought to be relevant are:

- the Supply of Goods and Services Act 1982, which deals with the care and standards of service, provided (as in section 8.4); and
- the Bills of Exchange Act 1882, for financial service providers this is very important as it relates to the cheques and payments of funds from customers' account.

There is also the issue of negligence (professional negligence will be covered more fully in the next section) and in the legal sense this is different to the common usage of the word, ie something which has unintentionally gone wrong due to somebody doing something wrong. If a customer wishes to prove that his/her financial services provider was negligent then they would have to prove that:

- a duty of care existed; *and*
- there has been a breach of that duty; *and*
- some loss or damage has been sustained as a result.

There is however the possibility of 'contributory' negligence where a plaintiff claims for compensation, however the claim is reduced because both parties have been considered to be negligent. Such an example may be where a customer inadvertently allows a third party access to his security codes and this third party uses this information to obtain account details from the contact centre.

The customer has a duty to provide their financial service provider with accurate personal information. This is particularly important when a new product is taken or a new account opened. The are a number of checks that providers make when they open an account for a new customer and the customer should be truthful at this stage as it forms the basis of the new relationship. These checks are as follows.

- *The customer needs to be able to identify themself* – either by supplying a passport or driving licence and every organization has its own guidelines on this. This is because the financial services provider has an obligation to try to reduce financial crime. By making a clear identification of a customer at the start they can help avoid fraud. If a provider opens an account for a fraudster who is passing stolen or forged checks or opens accounts for individuals who move large amounts of cash through the banking system to support criminal activity such as drug trafficking (this is known as money laundering), they are increasing the overall cost to the banking industry of controlling this type of criminal activity. This will impact on the customer in higher charges for services. Customers should remember that whilst two forms of identification, for example, might appear unnecessary, these guidelines are in place to protect the general public.

- *The person must be able to prove that they are fit and proper to open an account.* The financial service provider can usually check this through a credit reference agency search for bad debts and county court judgments. This will provide an indication of how this person conducts their financial affairs although there are occasions where customers have repaid the debt and it has not been removed from the records. The customer is able to access this information about them for a small charge directly with the credit reference agency.

- *The person must be able to prove they have the authority to open the account.* An example is where a fraudster obtains cheques payable to a company and opens an account in the company name purporting to be a director. The cheque is paid in and before usual checks are completed the fraudster withdraws the funds and is never seen again.

The financial services provider is within their rights to refuse a customer's account if they so wish. This cautiousness at account opening stage is because if the provider were to accept cheques into an account of someone that did not have rightful ownership of them, the rightful owner of the funds could sue the provider for 'conversion' of these funds.

8.6 Duties and rights of the organization and its employees

The account form that the customer completes forms the basis of the contract with their provider and sets out the terms and conditions. Financial service providers for banking services have a number of duties and rights to their customers once the contractual relationship is entered into, and these are outlined as follows.

- **A duty of care as an agent** – the provider acts as 'agent' for its customer when it pays or collects cheques on behalf of a customer and it owes a duty of care. A provider may be liable to a customer if its pays on a forged or altered cheque.
- **A duty of care as a trustee** – the provider owes a duty of care to the beneficiaries of a trust. It is not liable as a trustee unless it has been appointed as one.

- **A duty of confidentiality** – the provider owes its customer an implied duty not to divulge information about them to a third party, it must keep the affairs of its customers secret. Sometimes the provider will have to divulge information under compulsion of law, which may be in relation to alleged fraud or money laundering offences committed by the customer.
- **Banker's opinions or status enquiries** – occasionally providers will ask each other for 'opinions'. This could be on behalf of customers or on behalf of itself, where perhaps it has been approached to take over a mortgage commitment and the lender wants to check with the existing provider how the mortgage account has been conducted. This type of enquiry would normally require the customer's consent.
- **Duty of safe custody** – one of the traditional services provided by banks was to hold customers' property in their safekeeping usually in part of the cash safe. Any bank accepting such property has a duty to take care of it. If the bank allowed it to be lost or stolen it could be liable for breach of contract.
- **Banker's lien** – this means that a provider can sell off any securities (stock and shares) in its possession if a customer has no means to repay an overdraft. This does not include items held in safe custody.

We have seen above that bankers have a duty of care to their customers in addition to any contractual obligations and this raises the point of professional negligence. This duty will be considered in the light of the level of knowledge possessed by the customer in the event of a complaint and a higher standard of care is expected where the customer is vulnerable, ie where the expected level of knowledge of the customer is low. This is particularly relevant when considering advice given on financial service products.

In considering the standard of care required, a court tasked with a complaint for negligence would take into account the current accepted procedures of similar professionals and the extent to which the professional person in question adhered to them. Other considerations of the court will include an assessment of the risk to which the client was exposed and the protective steps which the professional would have taken and whether, or to what extent, these steps were taken to minimize risk.

An area that would be of interest to building societies and mortgage lenders is one that illustrates the example of professional negligence in relation to property valuations. It has been established by case law that a valuer who prepares a valuation report for a lender, to enable the lender to decide whether or not to lend on the property, has a duty of care to the prospective purchaser. If the lender employs the valuer, then by the principle of 'vicarious liability' the lender is also liable. In one case that went to court, a first-time buyer purchased a property with a mortgage and subsequently discovered a substantial fault with the property. The valuer was held to have a duty of care to him and was therefore liable. To emphasize the point about standard of care considerations, in another similar case, the valuer was not held to be liable simply because the purchaser was an estate agent and was expected to have a greater level of knowledge than the average member of the public.

To protect customers in their banking relationship and to set clear guidleines of conduct that customers can expect the Banking Code, was formulated in 1992. It was originally devised by the British Bankers Association, the Building Societies Association and the Association for Payment Clearing Services. It sets minimum standards for financial service providers in their dealings with personal customers. A personal customer in this instance is defined as a private individual who holds an account or uses services offered by that financial services provider. The account can be a joint account with another private individual or the customer, as an executor or a trustee, may hold it.

The Banking Code is monitored by the Banking Code Standards Board. It is an independent organization that makes sure that organizations that subscribe to the Code follow it and can take action if they fail to do so. Not all organizations subscribe to the Code, however for customers that choose a provider that does subscribe, it gives extra confidence in that organization.

The Banking Code sets out the key commitments and responsibilities that organizations promise to follow. A provider will make the following assurances to customers.

1. Act fairly and reasonably in all our dealings with you by:
   - making sure all our products and services meet the standards of the Code;
   - having safe and reliable banking and payment systems;
   - considering cases of financial difficulty sympathetically and positively; and
   - making sure our products and services meet relevant laws and regulations.
2. Help you to understand how our financial products and services work by:
   - giving you information about them in plain language;
   - explaining their financial implications; and
   - helping you choose one that meets your needs.
3. Deal with things that go wrong quickly and sympathetically by:
   - correcting mistakes quickly;

- handling your complaints quickly;
- telling you how to take your complaint forward if you are still not satisfied; and
- cancelling any bank charges that are applied due to our mistake.
4. Publicize the Code, have copies available and make sure our staff are trained to put it into practice.

The Banking Code is updated regularly; the most recent edition came into force on 1 March 2003. It contains standards that cover:

- running customer accounts;
- interest rates, charges and terms and conditions and how customers are told about these;
- protecting account and personal customer information;
- lending;
- moving accounts;
- dealing with financial difficulties; and
- complaints.

If a customer wishes to make a complaint and having done so they will then be entitled to take their complaint to the Financial Ombudsman Service as described in section 8.4.

Under the Banking Code financial service providers are required to treat all customer details in the strictest confidence and not to disclose information to a third party without the customer's consent, unless there is an overriding legal requirement to do so. There are four situations in which disclosure is permitted:

- if the customer requests or consents to the disclosure;
- if the financial services provider is legally compelled to do so, examples being in connection with drug trafficking and the prevention of terrorism;
- if it is in the financial service provider's interest to disclose, for instance if the customer has defaulted on loan repayments, the customer is given 28 days' notice before the default is registered with a credit reference agency; and
- if there is duty to the public to disclose, for example if a customer is trading with the enemy at a time of war.

Employees should therefore take care not to disclose customer information inadvertently. They should not talk about customers' accounts amongst themselves outside work or to their friends and relatives. This also extends to taking documentation about customers off the premises and taking care to dispose of customer documentation in the correct way.

Until October 2004 the Mortgage Code provides protection to the mortgage customer. It was introduced for lenders in July 1997 and for intermediaries (mortgage brokers) in April 1998. This Code provides valuable safeguards for customers and aims to help them understand how lenders and intermediaries are expected to deal with their mortgage.

The role of the Mortgage Code Compliance Board is to ensure that customers are fully informed and adequately protected when taking out a mortgage. They ensure that all of the lenders and intermediaries registered with them adhere to the standards set out in the Mortgage Code. This is done through a comprehensive programme of compliance inspection and liaison visits that are conducted each year. Additionally 'mystery shopping' and other consumer research exercises are conducted to ensure that customers are receiving the full benefits of the Code's protection.

The Mortgage Code sets out:

- how mortgages should be arranged by lenders and intermediaries;
- what information customers should receive before committing themselves; and
- how a mortgage should be dealt with once it is in place.

There are three levels of service that a mortgage provider can offer and they should tell the customer at the outset which of the following levels they can give:

- *advice and a recommendation* on which of the mortgages they can provide is most suitable for the customer;
- *information on the different types of mortgage product* on offer so that the customer can make an informed choice of which to take; or
- *information on a single mortgage product only*, if only one mortgage is available or if the customer has already made up their mind.

In addition the Mortgage Code has ten main commitments. These say that lenders and intermediaries will:

- act fairly and reasonably with customers at all times;
- make sure that all services and products keep to the conditions of the Code, even if they have their own terms and conditions;
- to give customers information on services and products in plain language, and offer help if there is any area which they do not understand;
- help customers choose a mortgage to fit the customer's needs, unless they have already decided on their mortgage;

- help customers to understand the financial effects of having a mortgage;
- help customers to understand how their mortgage account works;
- make sure that the procedures that staff follow reflect the commitments set out in the Code;
- correct errors and handle complaints speedily;
- consider cases of financial difficulty and mortgage arrears (missed payments) sympathetically and positively;
- make sure that all services and products meet the relevant laws and regulations.

Only qualified advisers are able to give advice to customers (ie they must have one of the required qualifications such as CeMAP™). Those staff that are involved in generating leads should take care not to become involved in discussions with customers that could be considered advice unless they are qualified to give such advice.

Any organization under the Code must be a member of a recognized complaints scheme, such as the Financial Ombudsman Service, described in section 8.4, or the Mortgage Code Arbitration Scheme. This gives customers an extra level of protection as each of these schemes can award compensation of up to £100,000 to customers if they suffer as a result of the lender or intermediary failing to keep to the Code.

From 31 October 2004 the Financial Services Authority (FSA) will be responsible for regulating the activities of lenders and intermediaries, who will have to follow the new rules in relation to selling and promoting first mortgages secured on the borrower's home.

The new regime will mean that the Mortgage code, which has provided a form of voluntary regulation since 1997, will no longer be required. It will be replaced by the Mortgage Code of Business Rules (MCOB).

The FSA will now regulate the sale and administration of those mortgages that meet the definition of a 'regulated mortgage contract', ie one that satisfies each of the following criteria:

- the lender is providing credit to an individual or trustee;
- the borrowers obligation to repay the loan is secured by a first legal mortgage on land (other than a timeshare) in the UK;
- at least 40% of that land is used, ie intended to be used, or as in connection with a dwelling by the borrower or by a related person.

Contracts that were entered into before 31 October 2004 cannot be subsequently regarded as regulated mortgage contracts, even if they satisfy the criteria.

Second charges and loans to companies are excluded from MCOB.

The MCOB rules cover such areas as:

- conduct of business.
- advertising and selling of mortgages.
- documentation relating to mortgages such as key facts, illustrations and other letters.
- how to calculate annual percentage rate.
- responsible lending
- charges
- arrears and possessions

Students are advised to make themselves fully aware of the new rules and understand the impact on their roles.

8.7 Summary

As the scope of banks' and building societies' activities has widened and the differences between them blurred, it has been necessary for the financial services industry to supplement legislation that governs customer relationships to ensure confidence in the industry. Whilst customers have a duty to supply accurate information about themselves and conduct their accounts in a reasonable manner, providers also have an obligation to present their services in a clear and transparent way and to treat their customers with respect.

To ensure that customer confidence is maintained at all times, the Banking Code and Mortgage Code lay out what customers should expect and what provides should undertake to do in the provisions of their services. This backed up by the Financial Services Authority and it is clear that these Codes will continue to drive the minimum quality requirements for the industry.

It is important that employers are aware of regulation of the relevant Codes and how these impact on their roles. The Codes have been devised for sound business reasons and advisers need to be aware of this in their day-to-day roles.

Unit 9

Customers and their protection

The aims of this unit are to enable you to:

- explain the need to protect customers, organizations and employees;
- state the types of customer and the differences between them;
- explain the data protection legislation and what this means for organizations and employees;
- describe the telephone preference service and the impact on contact centre operations.

In the last unit we covered the basic principles of law, contract and agency law, and the remedies available under each of these types of law. We then went on to discuss some of the specific protection afforded to customers within the financial services industry, in particular the procedure for customer complaints and how the Financial Ombudsman Service can assist a customer if they feel the response from their provider about their complaint is unsatisfactory. We looked at the Banking Code and Mortgage Code, which are backed by powers of the Financial Services Authority, and how these have been put in place to protect customers in their dealing with providers. We also saw how customers have a duty towards their financial provider primarily in providing accurate information on which decisions are based and behaving in a trustworthy manner.

This unit discusses the need for protection in more detail and the potential risks that are faced by the customer, the organization and its employees. In examining the customer further we will determine the different the types of customer, eg personal, business, clubs and charities and minors and some of the implications of these differences.

Finally we will look at two more aspects of customer confidentiality. The Data Protection Act 1998 binds all organizations so they need to be aware of its implications. Customers also have the option of registering with Telephone Preference Service in relation to outbound sales activity and we will look at the impact this has on contact centre operations.

9.1 Protecting stakeholders

In Unit 1.1 we said that stakeholders are the different groups of people who have an interest in an organization and its activities. In this section we will focus on customers, the organization and its employees.

If there is a need for protection for these three groups then this implies that there must be some form of risk.

Question

What are the risks to customers in their relationship with the financial services provider and its employees?

The potential risks to customers in their relationship with the financial services provider and its employees could be any of the following:

- poor advice leading to financial loss;
- failure of the service – whether this is through insufficient staffing, website failure or systems downtime;
- fraud on the customer's account for example from lost or stolen credit cards or information given out to fraudsters;
- errors on the customer's account.

No doubt there are several more that could be added to this list. In order to maintain confidence in the financial services industry various pieces of legislation have been enacted in relation to financial advice as well as regulatory rules and guidance such the Banking and Mortgage Codes discussed in the last unit. These exist for the protection of customers and whilst customers may sometimes feel that the some of the associated processes are rather long-winded and time-consuming it is for their own benefit in the long run. Organizations need to ensure that any systems have a back-up and disaster recovery plan as loss of service would be inconvenient for customers at the very least and would not instil confidence. The reputational risk, say, of the payments system going wrong would be immense, not to mention the cost of putting matters right.

Fraud on an individual customer's account can be very traumatic for a customer and many organizations carry safeguards to ensure early detection, particularly on credit card accounts. If an adviser were to give out information to a party that was not entitled to it, whether this led to fraud or not, this would be very serious. Errors on customers accounts made by advisers also raise the issue of reputational risk and customer confidence in the organization.

Question

What are the risks to organizations in operating their business?

There are a number of risks to organizations in operating their business. These may be:

- **financial risk** – this could be relating to the amount of reserves they have, shareholder funds they are using and ensuring that there is sufficient cash to fund day-to-day activities;
- **resource risk** – this could be relating to the labour supply, are there enough people of the right quality for each of the operation's premises, is there sufficient management time, is there sufficient training available for the people and are the buildings themselves fit for purpose?
- **regulatory risk** – as we have seen the financial services industry is subject to a high degree of regulation, whether from government or from the Financial Services Authority and associated bodies. There can be significant fines imposed on organizations that breach the rules;
- **reputational risk** – if something does go wrong there is always a

danger of adverse press comments and the impact this has on the organization's standing within the business community and the public.

An organization has a 'corporate social responsibility', which means it manages all the organization's risks to the benefit of society as a whole. This means that management should conduct their business in a fair and reasonable way and act in a way that does not prejudice the interests of any of the stakeholder groups.

Question

What are the risks for employees undertaking their roles in the financial services industry?

There are a number of risks for individuals who work in the financial services industry and these will also be dependent on the area in which they work. These risks could be:

- **breaching the regulatory frameworks** – advisers must ensure that they are suitably qualified to give any advice and not be drawn into giving advice when they are not qualified to do so;
- **customer confidentiality** – it is important for advisers to ensure that customers are identified properly and that they do not unwittingly give out customer information to a third party who is not entitled to it;
- **fraud and money laundering** – advisers are under a duty to report any instances where they are suspicious. Aiding a criminal in money laundering could result in the adviser being personally liable and subject to fines or imprisonment;
- **errors on customer accounts** – advisers have to take care that they undertake processes relating to customer accounts and information correctly. Continued errors could lead to coaching for underperformance. Advisers need to ensure that the quality of their work complies with what the organization expects of them.

Many of these risks can be overcome with the correct training and monitoring by an adviser's line manager. Line managers are responsible for ensuring that their advisers are sufficiently competent and receive the right level of support for the role that is being asked of them. Many of the authorized seller roles (eg for investment, insurance and mortgage advice) are underpinned by regulatory requirements and the needs of the Financial Services Authority. For an organization to be able to keep its 'authorized' status it has to show that any advisers engaged in this activity are fully competent to do so and receive the appropriate levels of training.

A further issue with selling is that some customers do not want to be approached via telephone canvassing and there are safeguards in place to protect these customers that must be observed. There are various other Acts and guidelines that cover these issues and we will go on to look at two of them, The Data Protection Act 1998 and the Telephone Preference Service, later in this unit.

9.2 Customer types

In Unit 6 we looked at segmenting customers into different groups for marketing purposes. In this unit we will look at how customers are grouped in relation to some of the legal aspects of the way in which customer accounts are operated and how organizations manage risks in dealing with them. For this purpose there are four main customer groups.

Question

What are the four main types of customer groups?

The different types of customers are:

- personal;
- business;
- clubs and charities; and
- minors.

It is also useful to group these customer types together for purposes such as commission charging structures, interest rates charges and product ranges. We will take each of these in turn.

9.3 Personal customers

Personal customers are any private individuals who can either have sole accounts – where a customer holds an account in their own name only – or joint accounts – where two or more customers hold an account together. If the account is in joint names then the customers signs a 'mandate' or authority form that sets out the signing instructions and liability on the account should it become overdrawn. Usually joint account customers are 'jointly and severally' liable on overdrafts. This means that if they default on the borrowing that the bank can pursue one or all of them for the debt.

There are various sorts of accounts that personal customers can open.

- *A current or cheque account* – this will have features such as a cash card or debit card, allows direct debits and standing orders, a cheque book with a cheque guarantee card, an overdraft and interest on credit balances. There are many different types of current accounts offered depending on the segment of the market they are aimed at. These segments will usually be students', graduates, mass market and premier customers.
- *Savings accounts* – these usually have a variety of features linked to interest rates. For example those accounts with a longer notice period for withdrawal of funds carry higher interest rates and often those accounts that are purely Internet-based carry better interest rates as the customer does most of the work in maintaining them so saving the organization from additional cost.
- *Loan accounts* – often customers will want to borrow money for purposes such as holidays, a new car or some other personal expenditure. Many providers will set up loan accounts that have a structured repayment schedule over a set period of time with the repayments coming from their current account. The Consumer Credit Act 1974 governs most personal lending up to £25,000. Providers have to ensure that advertising, quotes and agreements are drawn up in accordance within the regulations made pursuant to the 1974 Act.

There will be many other products linked to these accounts that financial service providers will offer as part of their product range. These may be credit cards, mortgages, life assurance, general insurance and so forth. There is a proportion, however, of the population that do not have bank accounts because they have a poor credit history or feel that they cannot afford the charges if something goes wrong. Most banks will decline personal customers if they are an undischarged bankrupt, have a record of fraud or have records of bad debts. A new type of account was set up for from 2003 this type of personal customer called the 'basic bank account' which has limited features for those people that want a simple account with no cheque book, so that they feel it is easier to keep control of their spending. Many of the main high street providers offer this type of account (for example the NatWest Step account, Lloyds TSB's Basic Bank account).

9.4 Business accounts

Banking for any legitimate business is a necessity. There are three main types of business that have fundamental differences in terms of ownership and liability for debt.

- **Sole trader** – this type of business is where the customer owns their own business. They trade under their own name and so are personally liable for any debts. This probably the simplest form of business arrangement and suits many traders with a modest income. A sole trader is able to employ others to assist them in their business activities.
- **Partnership** – this is a group of people who run a business together, eg a doctors' practice, an accountancy or law firm. The partnership is not a separate legal entity but a number of individuals who are jointly and severally liable for the debts of the firm. The partners draw profit from the business as their remuneration however you may come across 'salaried partners', who are in effect junior partners who have no rights to the profit of the firm.
- **Limited company** – again this is a group of people running a business, however a limited company is a legal entity in its own right. This is known as being 'incorporated', which means that the directors of the company have certificate to prove that the company exists and is registered with Companies House. Shareholders actually own the company and directors are appointed to run it, along with other employees. In many small companies shareholders and directors may be the same people, however, for organizations of great size, such as those quoted on the Stock Exchange, this is not usually the case. If a limited company fails neither the directors nor the shareholders are liable for the debt. It is likely, however, that the shareholders will lose any moneys that they have invested in the organization.

The signing instructions and other activities relating to any of the above types of account are covered by a mandate (authority). It is important that these mandates are kept up-to-date as personnel join and leave organizations and the financial services provider could inadvertently be paying cheques signed by someone not recorded in their mandate.

Most financial service providers will segment business by 'turnover' (ie income) that is generated by the business in a financial year. This gives segment names such as 'small business' (typically turnover up to £1 million), 'corporate' (turnover £1 - £10 million) and 'large corporate' (turnover in excess of £10 million). These businesses benefit from many services such as additional current account services to assist with payments and management of funds, a relationship manager, business cards for staff, overdraft and loan facilities. Many banks will ask business customers for their annual audited accounts so that they can track how well the business is going, particularly if the customer is borrowing. It is important to ensure to check that the business can afford to repay the borrowing and will be able to continue doing so.

9.5 Clubs and charities

The Charities Act 1993 controls clubs and charities. The Act defines the way in which the organization operates. The club or charity set their own rules when the organization is created, which they then need to follow in the normal course of operation. The services offered are similar to that of business customers. All bank accounts, cheque books and so forth have to be in the club or charity's name. Signatories will be nominated and only those people will be able to sign cheques or deal with the bank. The way in which the account or other services is run will be governed by the rules of the club or charity.

Many clubs and charities are very large and can have turnover equal to a corporate business or even a large corporate business. All charities and clubs will be particularly keen to look for ways to keep costs down so that they can ensure that their funds can be used to further the aims of the organization. To assist the charity or club in this aim banks will often agree favourable terms. Many of these types of organizations will have a central head office of employed staff, however rely on a large volunteer network to undertake much of the work. Some have controlling officers that have been elected by the members and whilst they may be experts in their field, may not always be proficient at running a business. If this is the case then it may be necessary for the financial provider to ensure that this officer group have the right support they need to run the finances of the organization. Usually the officers of the club or charity are not personally liable for its debts should the business fail.

9.6 Minors

A 'minor' is a person who is under the age of 18. This type of customer is generally unable to enter into contracts, other than to pay for necessities, or contracts that are to their benefit, such as contracts of employment. This means that if a financial services provider was to lend money to a minor, they would not be able to recover any of these moneys should the customer be unable to repay. This means therefore that usually minors are not able to arrange overdrafts or loans. An exception may be that if someone (usually a parent or guardian) were to provide a 'guarantee' for the loan and become a 'guarantor'. This means that if the minor was unable to pay for any reason then the lender could pursue the guarantor for any outstanding monies.

9.7 Data protection legislation

The Data Protection Act 1998 regulates the use of personal information held on computers and within manual records. The previous Act of 1984 only offered protection to information held on computer. The Act works in two ways, it:

- gives individuals certain rights; and
- gives those that record and use the information certain guidelines to follow. These practices are known as the 'Data Protection Principles'.

Question

What does personal information mean?

Personal information is data about living and identifiable individuals. The information does not necessarily have to be sensitive and can be as little as a name and address.

The three key principles of the Act are:

- a customer has the right to know if an individual or company has information relating to them;

- the customer has the right to see that information and the company or individual holding such information has to reply to such requests within 40 days. The request may be verbal or written; and
- that the customer has the right to have information erased or corrected if appropriate. Compensation is available to individuals who suffer damage by incorrect use if their data, its inaccuracy or unauthorized disclosure.

When the Act makes reference to 'data controllers' it refers to those that control the manner and purpose in which the personal data is processed. Data controllers could therefore be in any type of company within the public or private sector, a partnership or sole trader, or indeed an individual. In order to demonstrate compliance with the Act each data controller must have a 'Data Protection Policy'.

The person responsible for administering and enforcing the Act is known as the 'Information Commissioner'. The Information Commissioner is an independent official appointed by the Queen and who reports directly to Parliament. The Information Commissioner's office deals with matters relating to the Data Protection Act for the whole of the UK. The Information Commissioner's mission is that:

'we shall develop respect for the private lives of individuals and encourage openness and accountability of public authorities.'

In addition to the Data Protection Act 1998 the Information Commissioner and his staff monitor information in relation to the Freedom of Information Act 2000 and the Privacy and Electronic Communications Regulations.

Any organization or individual that processes personal information is required to notify the Information Commissioner of that fact. The size of the organization is immaterial, what is important is the personal information that is held in relation to the business activities. Organizations that fail to notify the Information Commissioner may find themselves facing heavy fines in the Magistrates Courts or higher.

By following the Data Protection Principles of the Act, organizations will set themselves a set of operating practices for good information handling. The Data Protection Act has eight Data Protection Principles the need to be followed. These are that data is:

- *obtained fairly and lawfully;*
- *held only for specific and lawful purposes;*
- *relevant, adequate and only for the purposes for which it is required* – the

quantity of the data needs to be checked and monitored regularly to ensure this is being held for the purpose of the business and they do not hold too much data about individuals. For example a financial services provider will collect date of birth information from its customers. When a customer reaches 18 the organization will target them with marketing material for a credit card or personal loan, as they are no longer minors. Whereas other organizations will only need to know that their customers are over the age of 18 and have the capacity to contract;

- *accurate and where necessary kept up-to-date* – data controllers should only collect and retain information that is actually required and that is accurate. Data controllers need to ensure that inaccurate data is corrected as soon as possible;
- *not kept any longer than necessary* – data controllers should ensure that collected information is not held indefinitely. Data should be continually monitored and that data which is no longer required removed from the system. For example when a customer completes the payment of their personal loan and their relationship ends with the finance company, their details should be removed from the system that would automatically be sending marketing literature to them;
- *processed in accordance with the individual's rights* – data controllers that use personal information for direct marketing need to ensure that the individuals are aware of the fact. Data controllers have to allow individuals the chance to opt out of having their information used in this way. The Information Commissioner receives numerous complaints about organizations that have used personal data in an unfair way. In order to remain legal, data controllers should set up and maintain a list of all the individuals that choose not to receive marketing material. The list should be checked prior to any marketing campaigns being conducted;
- *kept secure* – security of data is a major issue for both the data controller and the individual customer. The onus is on the data controller to ensure that everything within their powers is done ensure that personal information is kept secure. There is immense damage that could be done to the individual customer if their personal information was disclosed or lost through inadequate security.

Data controllers need to ensure that only those employees that are permitted gain access to personal information of individuals. This can be achieved through a series of passwords that are issued to authorised personnel. To ensure against misuse, passwords should be changed on a regular basis. Procedure documentation should be set up that lists which employees are authorized to access information, why and for what purpose. Disciplinary procedures should be put in place for any employee that has been found to misuse personal information.

The prevention of accidental loss or theft of personal data must be treated as a serious concern by any data controller. Although companies can put in place procedures and passwords to deal with the general day to day issues of safekeeping of data, what about the unexpected, unanticipated events such as fire or theft? Organizations need to ensure that back-up copies of files are kept in secure, preferably in an area in which they are not normally used and that the actual computer system is physically secure;

- *transferred only to countries outside the UK that offer adequate protection* – data controllers are permitted to transfer data to countries outside of the European Economic Area (EEA). EEA countries are the European Union, Norway, Iceland and Liechtenstein). They will need to ensure that the data receives adequate protection in that country or that the individual has agreed to release of their information to that country.

We can see that the principles of the Data Protection Act 1998 require that data controllers process information in a fair way. That means that when information is collected from individuals the data controller is open and honest about what it will be used for and they must have a legitimate reason for processing it. Additionally they will need to explain what they intend to do with the information and who the information will be given to.

Complying with the Data Protection Act will help organizations limit complaints from the general public on how they process the information they hold about individuals. It is therefore in the interest of the organization that they understand the individual's rights and comply. It is important that employees are aware of these customer rights. Employees need to be able to recognize when a request for information is being made and that they deal with and act upon that request promptly.

9.8 Telephone Preference Service

Most companies within the financial services industry will regularly conduct some type of telesales or telemarketing campaigns. Some believe this to be the most effective way of keeping existing customers up-to-date with new products and services and of introducing themselves to new and potential customers.

It is now illegal for organizations to make direct contact with personal customers, whether existing or potential, that have registered a desire not to receive unsolicited calls. In 1995 the Direct Marketing Association (DMA) set up the Telephone Preference Service (TPS). The TPS was originally formed as a voluntary, self-regulatory scheme to control unsolicited telephone calls. The idea was to make it possible for the general public to register their desire not to receive unwanted telephone calls from organizations wishing to promote and sell their products and services.

In 1997, following the implementation of the Telecommunications Data Protection Directive by the European Parliament, the Department of Trade and Industry (DTI) and the Office of Communications (OFCOM) entered into public consultation. As a result in May 1999 the Telecommunication (Data Protection and Privacy) Regulations were launched.

Earlier in 1999, OFCOM invited companies to bid for the management of the scheme, which at that time was known as the Telephone Opt-Out Scheme. The contract was awarded to the DMA, who now manage the scheme under the TPS banner. The original legislation has been updated and now the relevant statute is the Privacy and Electronic (EC Directive) Regulations 2003.

Individuals can register free with the TPS to eliminate unwanted and unsolicited calls. Organizations that undertake any type of telesales or telemarketing activity have the ability to receive the details of those individuals who do not wish to receive this type of call by subscribing to the TPS. Additionally when an individual tells an organization that their calls are not welcome and they do not wish to receive further calls, the organization must comply with this wish and remove the customer's details from the call list.

Organizations must adhere to the individual's request within 28 days. Therefore all organizations that make telesales or telemarketing calls must ensure that they clean their list to ensure that they comply with the regulations. As part of their subscription to the TPS organizations have a monthly update of the individuals registered with the TPS, which the organization can use to update its call lists.

It is important that employees only use those names that have been cleared against the list. This may be the responsibility of the marketing department to prepare the lists, however, employees should understand that if a customer says they do not want to be contacted again that this information must be recorded and acted upon.

An individual has the right to complain about any organization that contacts them, if they have registered their objection. This can be done either direct to the Office of the Data Protection Commissioner, who is responsible for the enforcement of the Regulations, or with the TPS. Complaints received by the TPS will be investigated by them and a full report filed at the Office of the Data Protection Commissioner.

The 'opt-out' register does not just apply to telephone contact and as contact centres are multi-media entities it is important to appreciate the other preference services available. These are:

- SMS messages – since 11 December 2003 it is unlawful to send unsolicited SMS marketing messages to an individual;
- silent calls – this is where the phones rings but there is no one there. These calls are generated by contact centre automatic dialling equipment when it dials more numbers then there are operators;
- mailing preference service – this can prevent unwanted direct mail posted to an individual's home;
- fax preference service – at the same time as the TPS legislation was launched in 1999 it was also made unlawful to send an individual an unsolicited sales and marketing fax without prior permission. Businesses also have the opportunity to register fax numbers on which they do not wish to receive direct marketing faxes.

No doubt with the growing number of e-mail Spam messages there will at some point be similar service that regulates sales and marketing over the Internet. Despite this, there will always be issues with regulating unwanted e-mails from foreign countries that are outside the jurisdiction of UK and European law.

9.9 Summary

There are a variety of risks that stakeholders can be exposed to and protection can be afforded to help mitigate these risks. Different types of customer carry different risks for the organization and it is good practice for the organization to put checks and procedures in place to cover any problem areas.

Data protection legislation has helped customers gain access to information that organizations hold about them and to ensure that none of their personal information is used in a way that would be detrimental to them. The

Telephone Preference Service, and associated preference services, control the ability of organizations, stopping them contacting individuals who do not wish to receive telesales contact. This again protects customers who do not want this type of intrusion.

Index

Index